Bicycling

Bicycling

Nancy Neiman Baranet

South Brunswick and New York: A. S. Barnes and Company
London: Thomas Yoseloff Ltd

© 1973 by A. S. Barnes and Co., Inc.

A. S. Barnes and Co., Inc.
Cranbury, New Jersey 08512

Thomas Yoseloff Ltd
108 New Bond Street
London W1Y OQX, England

Library of Congress Cataloging in Publication Data

Baranet, Nancy Neiman.
    Bicycling.

    Bibliography: p.
    1. Cycling. 2. Bicycles and tricycles. I. Title.
GV1041.B33   796.6   77-37803
ISBN 0-498-01051-1

First printing April, 1973
Second printing April, 1974

Jacket Photo Courtesy Gene Portuesi's Cyclo-Pedia

Printed in the United States of America

Dedicated to God, and
to all the families and friends
who cycle in the greatest country
in the world.

Contents

Preface

It's been said that the wheel is probably man's greatest invention, and the bicycle, probably the happiest application of that invention. Certainly, it is one of the world's best known means of transportation. In the United States, bicycling is now recognized as the nation's leading outdoor participation sport, with more than 44 million bicycles being ridden by over 62 million Americans.

While most American cyclists—probably nearly 80%—are youngsters, there are a few of us old die-hards who have refused to part with our youthful pastime, and have gone on to develop it into a lifetime sport and recreation.

In chapters to come I'll touch on the sports angle briefly, since it was a marvelous experience for me, and one that I recommend to all athletes, but for the most part, I'll try to expose the reader to the wonderful world of adult recreational cycling, for fun, good health and fitness; an activity that, once learned, is never forgotten; that provides the opportunity for "togetherness" and kinship, as well as a blessed alone-ness—communion between man, machine and nature. Cycling can be a beautiful, refreshing and exhilarating experience, and one that fosters harmony between man and machine, one of life's unique treasures.

Recreation cycling got its biggest boost in recent years when Dr. Paul Dudley White, the famed heart specialist, publicly proclaimed his theory that regular cycling could help prevent heart disease . . . that cycling could be an antitoxin to the "poisons" of living the easy life.

How many of us indulge in the electric-god inventions of the dishwasher, can opener, rideable lawn mowers, washer, dryer, vacuum cleaner, garbage disposal—to name a few—and on into the greatest family controller of them all, the automobile? While making living easier and certainly more pleasant, these marvelous items have nearly negated the necessary physical activity required to stay healthy in this 20th century. Think of the over-30 Saturday and Sunday sporting bloods who rise from bed to establish command of the boob-tube for at least 2 1/2 games each day with beer or soda-pop and chips as "involvement in action" companions. It certainly is little wonder that women control the greater percentage of wealth from husbands who have died eyes wide open, glass in hand and chip in mouth. And just remember, little eyes are watching! Nothing is a greater motivator of those busy little minds called children than examples set by us great all knowledged procrastinators called parents.

Where do we turn when the local gym teacher calls to relate that Junior has flunked the broad jump, the rope climb, the baseball throw, and constantly sinks to the pool bottom? Sad to say, many schools have had to lower the standards of their physical education programs because of parents who complain of the rigid requirements, rather than raising their standards to meet efforts attained by children who find athletics a family-oriented program.

Granted, there is no "fountain of youth" for any of us, and in spite of all the Madison Avenue media that constantly proclaims the secrets to eternal vivaciousness, the only reality is applied effort. I don't mean hours of endless training that go toward making a champion, but a consistent daily program that incorporates available time with all other responsibilities of life. However, we'll get to the "programming" later.

Bicycling

"Celerifere"

1
History of the Bicycle

For the real cycling buffs, some history of the equipment and the sport itself has to be included. If you don't enjoy a little knowledge from the past you can skip onto the basic material, but you might be missing a chuckle or two.

There are myriads of bicycle contraptions. Some never got off the drawing table; others should have stayed there. If you have the time to hit the used book stores, you might pick up a copy of Arthur Judson Palmer's *Riding High*, published by E. P. Dutton and Company, Inc. It's the most complete book I've ever seen on the bicycle's birth and its many side ventures in development.

Recognition for the first invention of a bicycle "type" is given to a Frenchman, Comte de Sivrac, who in the late 1790's constructed a crude form consisting of a carved wooden bar with padded saddle and two wheels. Known as an eccentric, de Sivrac gave it the form of a wooden horse. It was without a front fork so it couldn't be steered, and movement was initiated through the rider pushing with his feet like a baby in a walker. It was first called "Celerifere" and later became known as "Velocifere." It must have been great for coasting down cobble-stone roads!

However, around 1816, a German forester, Baron Karl Von Drais, constructed a similar vehicle to aid in his inspection tours. The Baron added a fork for the front wheel which allowed the rider to steer. It was called the "Draisine," or "Hobby Horse" and probably considered a great asset to the avid cobble-stone coaster. In 1818 Drais took the machine to Paris and created a sensation, and a whole new way of enjoying life.

The "Draisine" was then introduced into England in that same year by carriagemaker Denis Johnson, whose improved version added an adjustable saddle, rest for forearms, a different handlebar arrangement, and even a dropped

Ladies' "Draisine" Model

frame to accommodate the ladies costume. Contemporary lithographs show that this machine made such a hit with the "well-to-do" that rides through the countryside competed with exhibits at newly developed riding academies. Picture the top-hatted, tight pantsed, satin-tailed dandies "tippy-toeing" in a Madison Square Garden atmosphere for all the ladies to admire.

Since anything really athletic was frowned upon for the women of that era, a tricycle type

"Draisine"—Courtesy Smithsonian Institution

of machine was developed that operated by a push-pull, hands-and-feet movement. Beautiful and homely damsels, fully clothed in velvet, ribbons, whalebone corsets and ostrich feathers probably put forth a good deal more effort in making this nightmare move, than did the toe-dancing dandy on his padded plank.

Thankfully, in 1840 Kirkpatrick Macmillan, a Scottish blacksmith, was the first to use a leverage attachment to the rear wheel axle of a velocipede, beginning the self-propulsion system and ending the cobbler's shoe repair bonanza. The sight of this original idea in action caused such a commotion in the streets that Macmillan was promptly arrested.

But it wasn't until the 1860's that pedals were actually fitted to the front wheel axle by either

Ernest Michaux, or his employee, Pierre Lallement. Lallement emigrated to New Haven, Connecticut, and on November 20, 1866, obtained a patent (#59915) for a similar machine. It was listed as "improvement in velocipedes," but lovingly became known as the "boneshaker." The "improvement" revealed a spring mounted saddle that probably gave the effect of a vibrating rubber band—but consider the alternative. Chiropractors were surely sorry to see the demise of the original "boneshaker."

The Hanlon brothers of New York City obtained a patent for another improved version of the Lallement bicycle. It listed adjustable pedals and seat. They also suggested that rubber rings be used on the wheels to make them noiseless and prevent their slipping on the slick streets—the

"Hobby Horse School"—Courtesy Smithsonian Institution

Ladies Tricycle Type—Courtesy Smithsonian Institution

Macmillan Bicycle—Courtesy Science Museum, London, England

Ernest Michaux—Drawn by Charles Kreutzberger

Pierre Lallement—Courtesy Smithsonian Institution

forerunner, no doubt, to the tire. In 1869 they patented a mudguard over the front wheel, and a shoe brake that pressed against the wheel and was controlled by twisting the handlebars. However, the success of the old "boneshaker" didn't last long. It was awkward, extremely heavy and generally difficult to maneuver.

In order to accommodate the less physically endowed, one early inventor, S. H. Roper of Roxbury, Mass., made a steam operated velocipede. It appeared at fairs and circuses in New England in the late 1860's. It had the usual wooden wheels, iron band tires, and was propelled by the rear wheel, the axle of which was fitted with cranks connected to the steam apparatus. It was a forerunner of things to come.

In spite of this sidetrack for easy effort, big things were beginning to happen. In the early 1870's bicycles and tricycles began using wire wheels, and another English pioneer, J. H. Lawson, built an experimental rear-chain-driven safety bicycle. This rear chain safety bicycle was by-passed for a time, while the high wheeled bicycle, lovingly referred to in my circle as the "penny-farthing" (penny for the big English penny, farthing for the tiny English 1/4 cent piece) became the most popular idea at the turn of the century.

The Avril, first produced in England and then introduced to America by English firms exhibiting at the Centennial Exposition in Philadelphia in 1876, became known as the "ordinary" and was the first really practical bicycle. The rider was able to use the downward thrust of his legs in a reasonably effective movement. Compared to our "boneshaker," the "ordinary" was a lightweight, comfortable machine—and the key to a whole new industry.

When the Exposition closed, the unsold ordinaries were bought by the newly organized Cunningham Company of Boston, which in 1877 became the first bicycle importing firm in America. However, the financial geniuses saw the great popularity and interest that cycling was creating and refused to be content with importing old world products. Only the fire-arms industry predates the bike industry as a "mass-production" industry.

Col. Albert A. Pope took the first step in manu-

"Boneshaker"—Courtesy Schwinn Bicycle Company

Hanlon Brothers—Courtesy Scientific American

Roper Velocipede—Courtesy Smithsonian Institution

Avril "Penny Farthing"—Courtesy Scientific American

"Ordinary"—Courtesy Columbia Manufacturing Company, Inc.

facturing American bicycles under the trade name of "Columbia." The bicycle weighed over seventy pounds and cost $313.00. All this expansion took place in the factory of the Weed Sewing Machine Company, in Hartford, Connecticut, and by 1895, all of Pope's interests were concentrated in that city.

In 1877 *The American Bicycle Journal* was published in Boston, by F. W. Welson. It merged two years later with *The Bicycling World* and heralded America's first bicycle club, the Boston Bicycle Club. With the advent of industry, it was only natural for this area to become the center of cycling.

But the sporting interest didn't stay long in the East. The St. Louis Cycling Club of Missouri, organized in 1887, continues to educate, enlighten and assist both tourists and racers. It's the only cycling club in the world that has produced three generations of Olympic Team Members: 1928, Chester Nelsen, Sr., (Road Team) Amsterdam, Holland; 1948, Chester Nelsen, Jr. (Road Team) London, England; 1964, Donald Nelsen, (Pursuit Team) Tokyo, Japan.

Pictures in the 1880's show men standing beside their high wheeled "ordinarys" and "stars" before rutted roads. The bicycle is probably the biggest reason women got out of the kitchen, onto the roads and into womens' suffrage. The step from the kitchen to the ballot box couldn't have been

The Nelsen Family—Courtesy St. Louis Cycling Club Archives

Columbia Advertisement—Harper's Weekly

1880 Clubmen, St. Louis Cycling Club—Courtesy St. Louis Cycling Club Archives

Bicycle Sportsman—Courtesy Schwinn Bicycle Company

made otherwise. And if I ever saluted a really brave woman, it would have to be Amelia Bloomer, whose very feminine atmosphere shocked those who were looking for a freak at the public debut of her "bloomers." Amelia ended the era of the pale emaciated, tea-sipping fair maid, and began the era of the healthy, alert Gibson Girl. Who can ever forget "Daisy, Daisy, give me your answer do!"?

I have several marvelous *Harpers Weekly's* dating from 1886 to 1896, that illustrate the breathtaking accomplishments of cyclists. Advertisements show robust women, husbands and wives, young courting types, and straining athletes all enjoying this healthful exercise. Lithographs of riders carrying kerosene lamps for a night run, a bicycle race between a farmer complete with horse and buckboard and the mustached hero on a "penny-farthing" added to the penned displays of the latest equipment and specialized items.

A great deal of discussion of this "genteel" sport and its developing nemesis, the "Racing Scorcher," came out about this time. *Harpers Weekly*, under their "Amateur Sport" column in 1888, is quoted as follows:

There is no evil, just at the moment, to the correction of which sportsmen can address themselves

Gladiator Advertisement—Harper's Weekly

Amelia Bloomer—Courtesy New York State Library

Dayton Rider's Advertisement—Harper's Weekly

with such good purpose as the "scorching" bicyclist. The safety of pedestrians and the pleasure of the large class that rides the wheel but does not "scorch" demand the supression of this pestilent promoter of bicycling ills. Bent monkey fashion over low handlebars and chewing gum, as is customary with his kind, the "scorcher" speeds through the streets and along the park driveways reckless of consequence and indifferent to everyone's cheer, save his own.

With the interest of speed entering into cycling, safety was also to be considered and certainly the high wheeled "ordinary types" were not the safest. In the late 1880's the wheels were reversed with the rider sitting over the big rear wheel and using the tiny wheel in front. It was called the "Star" bicycle but it didn't prove to be any safer than the "ordinary." A fall from either seemed a disaster.

After many years of evolution, a return to the old hobby-horse type with two wheels of equal proportion led into the development of the so-called "safety" pioneered by J. K. Starley and H. J. Lawson. The "safety" was driven by chain or shaft to the rear wheel from pedals located well below the rider. The addition in 1898 of a coaster brake made by New Departure Company finally made cycling safe for the whole family. Our bicycles today are very much like this "safety," with the continuing additions of American inventiveness.

During the development of the "safety" there was another attempt, and a successful one as well, to incorporate a small steam engine and boiler. Lucius D. Copeland equipped a "Star" for self propulsion in 1885. It operated successfully, and two or three years later the Northrop Manufacturing Company of Camden, N.J., equipped a tricycle in the same manner for Copeland. Sanford Northrop issued brochures publicizing the formation of his Moto-cycle Manufacturing Company. Alas, it didn't succeed, but nevertheless was one of the many pioneer attempts in America that led toward the evolution of the automobile. German inventors Gottlieb Daimler and Karl Benz (I always thought his wife was Mercedes) are a part of the cycle-into-car development in history. Each produced, independently of the other, a gasoline engine powered cycle in 1885. Daimler's was a two

"Safety" Starley Rover—Courtesy Schwinn Bicycle Company

wheeled vehicle, Benz's a large tricycle with wire spoked wheels.

Pneumatic tires, although patented in 1845 by Robert William Thompson of England, really didn't come into wide use until 1888 when a veterinarian named John Boyd Dunlop from Belfast, Ireland, made tires for his son's tricycle. He patented the process the same year. In 1890 he began to manufacture bicycle tires and patented his invention in the United States on September 9 of that year.

Belfast would never be the same, and New York City had never seen the like, for this pneumatic tire was a part of the first six-day bicycle race in America, in the old Madison Square Garden, in 1891. Champion "Plugger Bill" Martin pedalled 1,466 miles and four laps in the six day event on his safety racer.

As the performances of the first cycling athletes improved, so did the bicycle itself. Practically every modern improvement in the automobile came from the evolution of the bicycle: pneumatic

Moto-Cycle—Courtesy Smithsonian Institution

Dunlop Advertisement—Harper's Weekly

Early 20's Sporting Enthusiasts—Courtesy St. Louis Cycling Club Archives

and cord tires, ball bearings, differential steering, seamless steel tubing, expansion brakes, gearing systems. Directly and indirectly, the bicycle influenced the imagination of those who went on to introduce the automobile.

Among these bicycle makers were: Henry Ford, Glen Olds, Charles Duryea, Alexander Winton, Albert A. Pope, H. A. Lozier and George N. Pierce, all of whom manufactured automobiles bearing their names. Note the Pierce bicycle dealership sign above the early twenties St. Louis Cycling Club wheelers, along with the carbide lamps and cobbled-stone road.

In addition, aviation pioneers Wilbur and Orville Wright and Glen Curtiss originally were bike specialists.

Once the bicycle clubs, touring clubs and cycling contingent associations were established, the next big step was speed records. On June 30, 1899, Charles M. (Mile-a-minute) Murphy rode on a wooden track laid between the rails of the Long Island Railroad. With the train as a windbreak, the measured mile was covered in 57 4/5 seconds. Murphy nearly met with disaster on the record ride when the special engine used for the event rocked the track. He was shaken out of his shelter

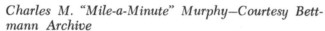

Charles M. "Mile-a-Minute" Murphy—Courtesy Bettmann Archive

and forced to challenge the buffeting wind drag. It was only with the greatest effort and difficulty that he brought his bicycle back into the protective haven; then at the end of the measured mile, the engine driver shut off the power too soon and Murphy ran into the train. The only saving grace was the pullman who caught Murphy and pulled him aboard.

In the 1880's Ohio's colorful speed king Barney Oldfield was bicycle racing champion of that state long before he began racing cars. Although he was out-classed in national competition, Oldfield's cycling career was highlighted again in 1902 when a young Henry Ford, seeking publicity for his horseless carriage, associated with Tom Cooper, another ex-bicycle racer to build the "999." Old "999" was a racing automobile that developed eighty horsepower, an extraordinary amount of power in those days. Neither Ford nor Cooper wanted to risk driving this speedster. Their search

for a fearless driver led to Cooper's former tandem bicycle partner, a man who thrived on speed, Barney Oldfield. Although Oldfield had never driven an automobile, he was eager to try. The two handed tiller that was used to steer the car fitted in with Oldfield's feeling for speed and the racing handlebar. On October 25, 1902 at Grosse Pointe, Michigan, Barney Oldfield won his first automobile race, outdistancing three contenders (one of the cars being driven by another ex-bicycle maker Alexander Winton) in a five-mile race to win the Manufacturer's Challenge Cup.

However, even automobile drivers never dreamed of forthcoming bicycle speed records. "Mile-a-minute" Murphy's record stood for forty-two years until May 17, 1941. Ex-six-day-bicycle-racer Alfred (Alf) Letourner designed a bicycle combination that had a front chainwheel with

Barney Oldfield and Henry Ford—Courtesy Ford Archives, Henry Ford Museum, Dearborn, Michigan

fifty-seven teeth, and a rear sprocket with six teeth. This inch pitch arrangement gave him a gear ratio of two-hundred fifty-two. With front fork reversed and a special small front wheel, Letourner was able to establish a close proximity to his wind break. This wind break had been installed on the rear of a midget racing automobile driven by famed auto racer Ronnie Householder. This combination broke Murphy's record by setting a startling measured mile time of 33:05 or 108.92 m.p.h. It took Letourner three miles to get over the 100 m.p.h. speed and four miles to slow down. Murphy's old train and track had given way to the more modern racing auto and a Bakersfield, California, expressway.

Jose Meiffret—Courtesy Photo Flammarion, Paris, France

Alfred Letourner—Courtesy Schwinn Bicycle Company

The fastest record to date, and one that should win any betting cyclist piles of money was set by Frenchman, Jose Meiffret. On July 19, 1962, near Freiburg, Germany, Meiffret pedalled behind a Mercedes driven by Adolph Zimber. The Mercedes was fitted with a wind break to shield Meiffret and a roller to keep the bicycle from rubbing the car itself. The bicycle was fitted with a monstrous chainwheel with 130 teeth and a sprocket with 15 teeth. The whole bicycle was reinforced to withstand the incredible stress, strain and torque. Meiffret wore the usual bicycle clothing with the addition of padded helmet. Because of the huge gearing combination (giving a ratio of 225 inches) a motorcycle had to be used to get the cranks rotating. At 20 m.p.h. Meiffret had

to struggle to gain control with his legs barely rotating. At 40 m.p.h. things became easier. At 50 m.p.h. he waved off the motorcycle and tucked in neatly behind the accompanying Mercedes. He also must have waved off some of the following possibilities:

1. If he did touch the roller bar at speeds in excess of 100 m.p.h. he could have lost control of the bicycle.
2. If he had come farther back than 18 inches out of his wind protection, the turbulence would have been the equivalent of hitting a brick wall and he would ultimately crash.
3. Centrifugal force might have caused either the wheels or frame to collapse.
4. Probably most eminent: any stone, dust, hole, crack or oil slick on the road could have caused him to lose control.

The course laid out allowed 4 miles to accelerate, the 1 mile stretch for timing, and 4 miles to decelerate. At the timing stations people could not comprehend the approaching energy mass. They saw the speeding car with an arched figure immediately behind, legs whirling, jersey shrieking. At the flag, the speed had increased to 127 m.p.h. Each revolution of the pedals carried him 190 feet and his legs were spinning at 3.1 revolutions per second. Meiffret knew he had to sustain this cadence for 18 seconds. When he passed the second flag, 6 timers for the International Timing Association registered 17.580 seconds, equivalent to 127.342 m.p.h. Meiffret, the Mercedes and the German Autobahn combined to establish a record that stands today.

These events are not representative of the true athletes in the sport. They're gimmicks, but believe me, the amount of bravery needed to attempt these trials makes every cycling athlete pause with head bowed, cap over heart and respectful prayer!

2

American Bicycling Racing History, International Level

American bicycle racing achievements in international competition have been meager. Although cycling has been a part of the Olympic Games since their revival by Baron Pierre de Coubertin in 1896, our only Olympic Gold Medal came in 1900 with a win in the 1,500 Meter Team Pursuit in Paris. The only other Olympic score was made by Carl Schutte, who won a third place Bronze Medal in the 200 Mile Unpaced Race, 1912, Stockholm, Sweden.

However, we have established some status for American cyclists in the annual World Championships. The great Arthur A. Zimmerman was outstanding. Only the "old timers" and record books remain to tell of the exploits of these great wheeling heroes, but those who heard the tales of Arthur Zimmerman, the "bicycle's Champion," always spoke of his sportsmanship and friendliness along with his victories. Although his training methods seemed to break most of the rules of keeping fit, his performances were always top notch crowd pleasers.

American World Championship Amateur Stars are:

1893 Chicago, Illinois
　　　Event
　　　1 Mile　1. Arthur A. Zimmerman
　　　　　　　2. John Johnson
　　　　　　　3. J. P. Bliss
　　　10 Mile　1. Arthur A. Zimmerman
　　　　　　　2. J. P. Bliss
　　　　　　　3. John Johnson

Arthur A. Zimmerman—Courtesy Amateur Bicycle League of America

1899 Montreal, Canada
　　　Sprint　D. Peabody (Second Place)
1900 Paris, France
　　　Sprint　John H. Lake (Second Place)
1904 London, England
　　　Sprint　Marcus Hurley (First Place)
1912 Newark, N.J.
　　　Sprint 1. Donald McDougall
　　　　　　　2. Harry Kaiser
　　　　　　　3. Dave Diver

Again, we had a long wait until 1949 when

Jack Heid took a Third Place in the Sprints at Copenhagen, Denmark.

Another twenty-year wait until 1968. Then in Montevideo, Uruguay, Jack Simes, III, placed second in the 1000 Meter Time Trial (Time 1:10.40).

John H. Lake—Courtesy Amateur Bicycle League of America

Jack Simes, III—Courtesy Louis Maltese

Jack Heid—Courtesy Al Hatos

In 1957, women's events were admitted in the World Championships and American women were given a chance to add their efforts to obtain recognition for our athletes. Our biggest boost came when Mrs. Audrey McElmury won the Women's Road Race and a Gold Medal at the World Championships in Brno, Czechoslovakia, in 1969. In 1972 Sheila Young won a Bronze third place Medal in sprints at Marseilles, France.

The outstanding fact about all these World Championship athletes is that they were amateurs, going over at their own expense to represent the U.S.A. against semi-professionals who are provided training camps, free equipment and gratuities for every performance or achievement.

At the Professional level, Americans certainly

Marshall W. "Major" Taylor

Audrey McElmury—Courtesy Al Hatos

held their own during the golden heydays of turn of the century cycling. Over 600 registered professional cyclists graced American audiences with hair-raising, precision timed performances. Today there isn't one.

American World Championship Professional Stars are:

1895 Cologne, Germany
      Event
      Sprint G. A. Banker—(Second Place)
1898 Vienna, Austria
      Sprint G. A. Banker—(First Place)
1899 Montreal, Canada
      Sprint 1. Marshall W. "Major" Taylor
               2. Nat Butler
1904 London, England
      Sprint Iver Lawson (First Place)
1912 Newark, N.J.
      Sprint Frank Kramer (First Place)

Frank Kramer—Courtesy Otto Eisele

These great stars all competed against each
other, first as amateurs, and then as professionals.
The outstanding "Major" Taylor was the first
Negro to win a World Championship. His auto-
biography "The Fastest Bicycle Rider in the
World," published by Wormley Publishing Company, brings to life the times and trials of these
professional heroes. Taylor was somewhat of a
Jack Armstrong type in his own right (no smok-
ing, no drinking) and an amateur poet as well.
Somewhat flowery, but really striking is his "Black
versus White":

> "As white as you are, and black as I be
> Speed is quite natural to me,
> For black as I am and white as you be
> My color is 'fast' black you see.
>
> As white as you are, and black as I be
> Still I'd rather be me.
> For black as I be and white as you are
> I may be whiter inside by far.

Nat Butler

As white as you are, and black as I be
Still it was nature's decree
For black as I be, and white as you are
I can be white though blacker than tar.

As white as you are, and black as I be
God created us both, and He
can best judge though black as I be
Who's the whiter inside, you or me?"

As the history of our athletes developed, so did the history of man and the bicycle. It met the need for inexpensive individual transport. Regretfully, for the health of our citizens, the majority use of the bicycle regressed to the toy stage, while less affluent Europeans continued to use it as an inexpensive method of transportation. It is interesting to note that when the economic status of a country rises, the consumer need for the bicycle recedes.

At the turn of the century, the adult use of the bicycle in the U.S.A. rose from an estimated 200,000 in 1889 to 1,000,000 in 1899. Today, 44 million bicycles are being ridden by 62 million Americans, with probably less than 20% being used by adults.

However, with the onslaught of extra time, money, and the realization that some physical activity has to be engaged in to keep healthy, there is a trend toward the increase of adult use of the bicycle. Neighborhood associations, touring clubs, bicycle hostelling associations that provide world wide cycling trips and local bicycle paths are making it possible for the whole family to get involved.

3
Buying a Bicycle

Buy a bicycle and get involved! Reflecting on this great number of bicycles that statistics show are available and ready for use, the immediate thought is: let's get on the child's bicycle and begin a wonderful cycling program that will bring back the elasticity in the lungs and the color in the cheeks! I can guarantee the reverse of this "dream" if the child's stock bike is dusted off.

Think for a minute. The fellow or gal who exercises by playing golf wouldn't think of taking the child's toys to a driving range, let alone a golf course. Or take the tennis addict: he wouldn't be caught dead at the nets with junior's plastic-coated look-alike. But why is it that every American assumes that the conventional bicycles the children use will benefit him more than any of the other toys.

The flashy dressed items that draw the child's attention to a particular sport toy are designed to appeal to a child. While I realize the capital outlay for the child's bicycle is far larger than for the cheap tennis racket or play golf clubs, the end result is the same. A toy is a toy is a toy! (No matter how long a seat post you've bought!) And before we start with "what to buy" let's start with something that's even more important: "where to buy."

Cycling is a specialist's field. The local department store, hardware store, discount house or automobile equipment shop cannot fill your needs. Although they do carry some sports and light-weight bicycles, they are generally sold boxed to the consumer. When they are sold assembled, they are seldom (if ever) put together competently. Today's bicycle salesman in the department store

might have been yesterday's swimsuit specialist. And most important, department stores never give service. They do not stock a complete supply of replacement parts, and if you buy a bastard model that's been imported from lower slobovia to meet a consumer demand for a cheap "look-alike," you can be sure it will not only fall apart, but also that the odd-ball equipment can never be replaced. So any imagined saving goes down the old drain when you have to replace those "look-alike" parts with a whole new bicycle.

Small things like adjustment of brake and gear cables, adjustment of the brakes and gears themselves, correct alignment of chain to derailleur gears, "trueing" the wheels to make sure they're round (just mentioning a few) are not a part of the department store's personnel abilities. And, naturally, how many salesmen can even fit a bicycle? If you're 6'4", you surely take a different frame size than the 5'10" individual.

Picture setting: Zimbel's Super-Sonic Department Wholesale Discount Store

Characters: Two Consumers (Husband and Wife) One Salesman

Act I—Scene I: Consumers enter department store.

Male: "Gee, that sure is a great looking bicycle!"

Female: "Gee, that sure is a great looking bicycle!"

Salesman: "Sure is! . . . and it sells like a VW!"

Male: "How fast will it go?"

Female: "The colors are lovely!"

Salesman: "A fellow like you could really burn up the road! . . . And it comes in 22 libidinous shades, and one universal size to fit both you and the missus.

(*Husband pulls in gut, throws leg over bicycle,*

leans over handlebars, grits teeth, says "roooommmm, roooommmm" . . . Wife busy checking color chart.)

Salesman: "It's really a great bicycle, and today's the last day of our special sale. I'll even throw in an extra long seat post for the Mister!"

(Small family conference.)

Male: "If you knock 10 bucks off the price, we'll take two. Make mine Linus White and hers Gregarious Green!"

Salesman: *(Pencil in hand scribbling, hands consumer invoice)* "Thank you very much! You can pick up your cartons at the dock; the instructions are right inside the boxes.

Male: *(Still on bicycle, but with slightly knotted brow)* "You mean I have to put them together myself?"

Salesman: *(Gradually easing away toward another inexperienced clod)* "It's really very simple; a child can do it, and you college grads can zip it together in a jiffy!"

(Male type puffs chest, female type looks admiringly at male type, salesman drifts off with a new "May I help you folks?")

Now, we won't even go into what happens at home. We'll just go back into the store two months later.

Salesman: "May I help you folks?"

Male: *(Producing invoice, waves it under salesman's nose)* "We bought two of those Zambezie-Etruscan specials two months ago. They've never worked right since we bought them. Now the gears won't work at all, the brake levers fall off, and the rear wheel on my wife's bicycle is oval. You've got to do something!"

Salesman: "Gosh, that's too bad! But it's been more than 30 days since you bought them, and we don't refund except for structural failure. Some customers aren't efficient enough to assemble them correctly, but that's not our responsibility. However, you college grads seldom run into that difficulty. I'm sure it's just a matter of adjustment. Why don't you take them to Gene's bicycle shop on the next block. I'm sure he wouldn't charge you too much for some minor adjustments. Can

you excuse me? I just heard my name over the PA."

(Flash to Gene's Bicycle Shop. . . . and four others in the City, with the same conversation ensuing in each. Enter our consumers pushing, carrying, dragging parts and bicycles.)

Male: "The salesman at Zimbel's said you do minor adjustments at a reasonable price. We just don't seem to be able to get these bicycles to work efficiently!"

(Gene and four others examine pile of debris.)

Gene: "Sorry, we only service what we sell. Take it back to where you bought it and ask for their 30 day free service."

Male: "But they don't have service!"

Gene: *(Gleam in eye, self-satisfied sneer on face.)* "Gee, that's too bad, isn't it?" I'll bet you even buy new cars without finding if there's service available! We do some general bicycle parts repairs, but there are no replacement parts in this country for those you've damaged."

Male: "What can I do?"

Gene: "Do come back when you need a new bicycle!"

Male: "Can't you tell me what to do? I'll fix it myself!"

Gene: *(Patiently, as to an idiot child.)* "It takes two and a half years to train a bicycle mechanic who gets $8.00 an hour. Five minutes of my time is worth $20.00. I'll take sixty seconds and tell you this. . . . you bought a bastard model look-alike from a discount house imported to sell for $10.00 less than what we bicycle dealers offer. Aside from the fact that the quality is inferior, there are no replacement parts or service available. In reality, the bike is worth $40.00 less than our model that retails for $10.00 more. Consider your purchase as one positive step toward your basic education. . . . 'Caveat Emptor.'"

That ends a small resume of *where not to,* and it should lend a little insight into *where to.* There could be an exception to the above rule-of-thumb where a really qualified person has been overlooked, but on a personal tour of twenty-two Detroit area department store and discount houses,

I was unable to find one.

Although it may sound like a "plug," I must give credit, where credit is really due. The Schwinn Bicycle Company trains its mechanics before they are given a dealership, so when you're looking for some special service this might be a point to remember.

There is for the cycling specialist the *Cyclo-Pedia Catalogue and Handbook*, 311 North Mitchell, Cadillac, Michigan, 48601. These people are specialists who stand behind their products and carry complete replacement equipment. They also handle many out-of-the-ordinary items that your local bicycle dealer cannot carry.

4
Types of Bicycles and Equipment Description

There are many bicycle designs available to the consumer:

1. The Stock Bicycle
2. The Utility Lightweight
3. The Sport or Club Bicycle
4. The Cyclo-Tourist or Camping Bicycle
5. The Mixte Bicycle
6. The Road Racing Bicycle
7. The Track Racing Bicycle
8. The Tandem
9. The Adult Tricycle

Now, as sure as God made little green apples, somebody's going to say, "Ah-ha! She forgot the ....!" The nine named above are the most popular, most functional, high performing or easily obtainable in this country.

One big, inescapable fact has to be recognized. The correct, proven and most functional design for a bicycle frame is the diamond framed "mens model." Actually, the men have no special claim to this design, it's just that the so-called "ladies model" with the missing top tube was really designed to accommodate a skirt.

There are valid reasons why a ladies' cycle or mixte frame is used, particularly if you're a very small adult and can't obtain a small enough diamond frame for you to get proper dimensions from saddle to pedals, or if you're in a community where the ladies model is used for transportation. Aside from these reasons, only the diamond frame should be considered. Fitting the bicycle to your measurements is discussed in Chapter 6.

Before we get into each of the nine bicycle designs, we need to have a basis for generalized communication. Those with a Ph.D. would call it bicycle nomenclature, but I like "Parts Chart."

Frame: The metal structure itself. Frame size in quality machines is now determined by the length of the seat-post tube, not the wheel size. Generally, centimeter size is used because it's universal, but it equals out to approximates of:

52 cm—20 1/2"
55 cm—21 5/8"
56 cm—22"
58 cm—22 7/8"
60 cm—23 5/8"
61 cm—24"
63 cm—24 3/4"
65 cm—25 1/2"

This enables the adult from 5'3" to 6'4" to have a proportionately built bicycle.

Frame Angles: The angles of the frame are determined by the angles of the seat tube and head tube, and can give either a softer-comfortable ride, or rigid performance ride.

Wheelbase: Wheelbase is determined by the distance from front wheel axle seating to rear wheel axle seating of the frame. Curvature of the front fork helps determine the wheelbase. A very short wheelbase (found generally on the track racing bicycle) is accentuated by a straighter fork, providing a much stiffer, rigid ride.

Lugs: Lugs are little collar-type extra pieces that help join the frame tube pieces to one another, so that welding the frame and heating

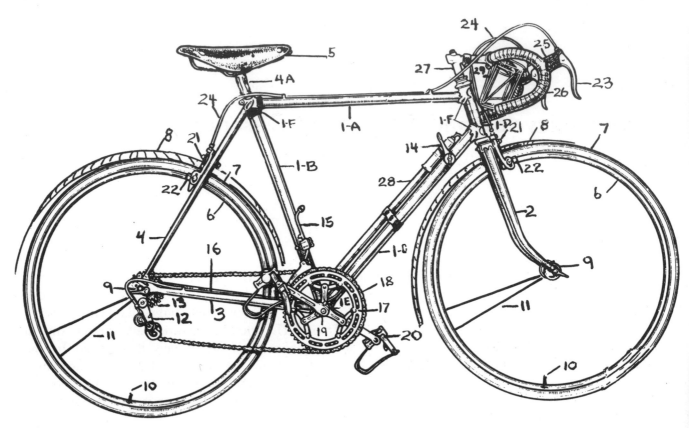

Parts Chart

1.	Frame	12.	Gearing Mechanism
1-A.	Top Tube	13.	Freewheel Block
1-B.	Seat Tube	14.	Gear Control Lever
1-C.	Down Tube	15.	Chainwheel Changer
1-D.	Head Tube	16.	Derailleur Control Cables
1-E.	Bottom Bracket	17.	Chainwheel
1-F.	Lug(s)	18.	Chain
2.	Fork	19.	Cranks
3.	Chain Stays	20.	Pedals, Toe Clips and Straps
4.	Seat Stays	21.	Brakes
4-A.	Seat Post	22.	Brake Blocks
5.	Saddle	23.	Brake Levers
6.	Rims	24.	Brake Cables
7.	Tires	25.	Brake Hoods
8.	Mudguards	26.	Handlebar
9.	Hubs	27.	Stem
10.	Tire Valves	28.	Pump
11.	Spokes	29.	Bottle Cage

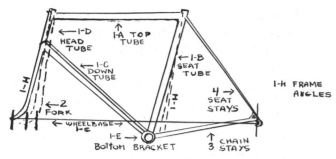

Parts Chart

Clincher Tire

Tubular Tire

the tubes to 2,800° is unnecessary. Brazing (low temperature heated from 1,600° to 1,800°) prevents the metal from fatiguing and becoming brittle through the use of excessive heat when joining the tubes. If the frame is not lugged, it is not a quality machine.

Lugged Frame Joint

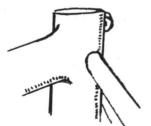

Welded Frame Joint

Fork: The fork is the part of the bicycle that holds the front wheel in the frame. Curvature of the front fork helps determine the wheelbase.

Rims and Tires: Rims are the metal structure for seating the tire. Tires, like rubber cushions are either:
A. Clincher Type (tube and tire separate).
B. Tubular Type (tube sewn into the tire).

Hubs and Spokes: Hubs are the pivoting-rotating center of the wheels. Spokes are the wire stabilizers that join the rim to the hub. Hubs are either:
A. High Flange, providing a more rigid ride.
B. Low Flange, providing a softer, more comfortable ride.

High Flanged Hub

Low Flanged Hub

Gearing Mechanism: The gearing mechanism is that marvelous invention that allows the rider to select the speed at which the feet will rotate. There are two types:
A. Derailleur Type: can be 5, 10 or 15 speed type. When activated by control lever on

the down tube, the chain can move up and down the sprocket block on the rear hub.

B. Hub Type: can be 3 or more speeds. When activated by the control lever located on the handlebar, the internal hub gear mechanism responds.

Sprocket Block: This is a combination of assembled sprockets attached to the rear hub that help determine the gearing combination in connection with the chainwheel. Teeth are 1/2″ spaced to match chainwheel.

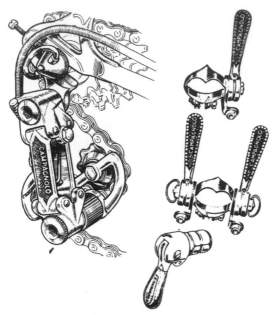

Derailleur Gear and Levers

Multiple Sprocket Block

Sprocket: The sprocket is the singular cog used on the rear wheel hub in connection with the chainwheel and helps determine the gear. It can have either 1″ spaced teeth or 1/2″ spaced teeth to match chainwheel.

Hub Gear

Singular Sprocket

Chain: The chain is the medium that receives thrust from the chainwheel and carries it to the rear sprocket or sprocket block. It is either 1″ pitch (spaced links) or 1/2″ pitch (spaced teeth), as determined by chainwheel and sprocket.

Half-Inch Pitch Chain

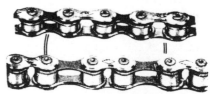

Hub Gear Lever

Inch Pitch Chain

Chainwheel(s) and Chainwheel Changer: The chainwheel is the circular metal indented disc that is turned when the pedals are rotated and activates the rear wheel through its medium, the chain. Either 3 pin or 5 pin to match crank, there are two styles:

A. Singular Chainwheel: Either 1″ spaced teeth or 1/2″ spaced teeth to match rear sprocket.

B. Multiple Chainwheels: 1/2″ spaced teeth to match rear sprocket block. The multiple chainwheel combination is operated by the Chainwheel Changer. It can be the manual type or lever mechanism. This changer moves the chain up or down the chainwheels, providing multiple gear combinations.

Multiple Chainwheels, Half Inch Pitch, Five Pin

Singular Chainwheel, Inch Pitch, Three Pin

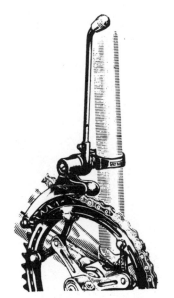

Manual Chainwheel Changer

Singular Chainwheel, Half Inch Pitch, Three Pin

Lever Controlled Chainwheel Changer

Cranks: Cranks are the extension media between the chainwheel and pedals. There are two styles, with some variation:

A. Combination crank and chainwheel welded together.

B. Separate cottered or special cotterless can be either three or five pin. Separate crank and chainwheels allow selection and change of chainwheels for specific gearing combinations. Choice of 3 or 5 pin cranks is arbitrary.

Pedals: Pedals are the leverage points that rotate the cranks.

Toe Clips and Straps: Toe Clips are spring steel guards that secure the foot directly on to the pedal. The straps are leather, and provide the tightening agent.

Brakes: Brakes slow or stop the bicycle. There are two types:

A. Coaster Brake: A rear hub brake that is actuated by reverse pedal action. Some coaster brakes are combined with a hub gear, generally found on the small-fry bicycles.

B. Rim Brakes—Center Pull: A caliper rim brake actuated by hand operated brake lever.

Combination Crank and Chainwheel Welded Together

Separate Cottered Three Pin Crank

Separate Cotterless Five Pin Crank

Coaster Brake

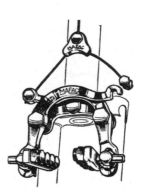

Rim Brake, Center Pull

Rim Brake, Side Pull

5

Bicycle Specifications and Specialized Equipment

Butted Tubing: Now, why butted tubing in the highly specialized bicycles? All bicycle tubes are hollow, and many grades of steel can be used for any ordinary bicycle. For most of these pipe is either rolled and sealed (seamed) or hollow formed and then chopped up in exact pieces for the correct bicycle size.

However, when the bicycle comes equipped with double-butted tubing (the gauge of the metal being thicker at each end where it joins the other tubes), a very high grade of steel alloy is used (manganese-nickel) which must be specially formed. It has to be a stronger metal because:

1. The joint (lugged area) is where the greatest strength is necessary. Between the lugs, the tube can be narrowed in its thickness (not in its overall diameter) for added lightness to the whole bicycle.
2. Butted ends bear heat fatigue during brazing or silver soldering with less fatigue or damage.
3. This high grade metal has a greater stress and recovery basis. Energy exerted by the rider is absorbed and transferred to the action of the bicycle. There is little "give-sag-whip-sluggishness."
4. Stress recovery is quicker. This means when the massive push and pull energy is applied by the rider and absorbed by the bicycle, the metal recovers faster for the next thrust. Consider what a metal like aluminum would do in this circumstance. Although it's vastly lighter, it would actually destroy itself by counter action-reaction.

Other items of bicycle nomenclature that need additional explanation for the laymen are listed and explored further because they're really necessary for *efficient* cycling, and their reason for being and application is easily understood.

The funny turned-down sports bar: Always, I hear. . . . "but I don't want to race!" The need for the turned-down bar has nothing to do with racing unless you want to race. It was designed from the experience of millions of miles of cycling. There are various designs in the turned-down bar, and both steel and alloy are used, but the basic sports bar design is a necessity. The usual "steer-horn" bar forces the cyclist into a push-push

Steer Horn Handlebar

Turned Down Sports Bar

movement of the feet, and into an upright position on the saddle that transfers all body shock to the spinal area. The sports bar lets the cyclist assume a slightly forward leaning position that transfers some of the weight off the spinal area, and allows the cyclist to rotate the legs. There are many styles with varying degree of drop and length of bar top.

When accelerating or climbing a hill, the rider with the sports bar drops his hand to the lower area of the bar and can continue to rotate the legs. The "steer-horn" bar forces the rider to stand on the pedals to accelerate or climb, and makes it impossible to use the added power of the arm, back and shoulder muscles in the circular thrust of the legs. Naturally, it might be uncomfortable at first because the position is new and strange, but it's efficient!

The Sports Saddle: The sports or racing saddle (excluding the track racing saddle) is the best. There are again many styles from which to choose. They are designed to let the powerful buttock and thigh muscles work freely. My own saddle, which I've had since 1952, is only 5″ wide at the rear, and 7″ of its total length of 11″ is only 1 1/4″ wide, yet I've ridden this saddle for twelve consecutive hours, pedalling 208.87 miles.

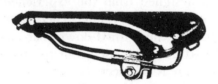

Sports Saddle

Spring Mattress Saddle

The wide spring mattress saddle looks like comfort, but it's worthless if you plan to develop any cycling proficiency. You can't afford to sit on 1/2 of your best muscles and have the other half rubbed raw at the side,

or have 2/3rds of all the energy you're expending absorbed by that mushy sponge. Again, the sports or racing saddle will take some getting accustomed to (for either sex) and it might "smart" a bit, but after six or seven weeks of use, try a quick jaunt on your friend's "mattress" and see how greatly your action is hampered.

Toe Clips and Straps: These, along with cycling shoes and cleats are another absolute necessity. By strapping the foot onto the pedal, the rider will never lose control of the bicycle from a foot that slips off the pedal. However, the most important reason is that a circular action of rotating the pedals cannot be developed without them. The plain shoe on a plain pedal can only push, push, push. That's 1/2 of the power available. *There is also pull.* While one leg is pushing, the other leg should be pulling up. This is finally refined into the beautiful rotational movement of the experienced cyclist. There are three sizes of toe clips, Small, Medium or Large. Since the most efficient foot position has the ball of the foot directly over the pedal as the power source, the length of the clip has to be determined before shoe cleats are nailed fast.

Derailleur Gears: It's useless to say "this make" or "that style" is the best. Style and design will always change and improve. My concern is that the derailleur's value and correct use is recognized.

One of the many advantages of the derailleur gear is its extreme flexibility in obtaining desired ratios. The cog block on the rear hub, and the front chainwheels can be selected or changed to fit the rider's physical capability in handling any terrain. The 3-speed hub type gear found on the utility cycle gives a low, medium and high gear. Always, the low is too low unless you're riding against a 30 m.p.h. wind, and the high is too high, unless there's a 5 mile straight downhill with a 30 m.p.h. tail wind. A second big drawback to the hub gear is the fact that the rider has to coast while shifting. Imagine this going uphill. The derailleur gear is shifted as the rider continues to pedal. While we're on why they're needed, let me discuss how to use them properly.

As a beginning cyclist, the temptation will arise to cycle in a high gear because:

A. "I go faster."

B. "I feel my feet are spinning too fast in a lower gear."

However, a beginning cyclist's reflexes are extremely sluggish and riding a high gear can cause excessive strain and fatigue on muscles not yet conditioned to the action.

What is a good gear? I can only give examples. The gears ridden are governed by mental and physical conditioning, as well as equipment you use. The gear that feels just right on the first spring ride is no longer your best gear after a month of cycling and several hundred miles. A general rule would be to start in a 60 or 70 inch gear.

High and low gear needs also depend upon the variation of the terrain. How many combinations . . . 5, 10 or 15? There again, it depends on how much you're really going to use that bicycle, and where you're going to ride it. If you just plan to cycle around the local flat cycle path, 5 speeds is really sufficient. If you're going to head out into the country and hills, you might need 10 or 15.

How to figure a gear? Take the diameter of the rear wheel in inches, multiply by the number of teeth in the front chainwheel and divide by the number of teeth on the rear sprocket.

Now, how to get the most out of your derailleur. Develop a smooth, fast and rhythmic cadence. This is accomplished by riding lower ratios than normal gears at the beginning of each season. If your pedal action is so slow that you are "pile-driving" at each stroke, or if your feet are going around so fast there isn't any resistance in the pedals, you'll have to adjust the gear because you're no longer cycling with efficiency.

Again, I have to mention toe clips and straps. It's impossible to develop cadence without them. You must be able to pull up with one leg while pushing down with the other, and it can't be done without the toe clips and straps.

For the average cyclist, cadence is the key to determining a practical gear. The most comfortable gear, under normal conditions, should be rotated at approximately 75 revolutions of the crank arm per minute. How to continue these r.p.m.s going uphill, downhill, with or against the wind, is developed through practice and use of the derailleur. When the rider begins to climb, it's natural for the cadence to begin to fall, and as the incline gets steeper, the pedal action decreases from 75 to 70 to 65, etc. The proper action now is to shift to progressively lower gear ratios until the cadence is back to approximately 75 r.p.m. When the downhill stretch comes, the rider shifts up into progressively higher gears to maintain the comfortable cadence.

Seventy-five r.p.m.s on a 70 gear would give 15.65 m.p.h. That's excellent and can be done easily. Seasoned groups travel at about 17 or 18 m.p.h.

As you improve and become more efficient, the cadence will develop to 80 and 90 r.p.m.s and you can review the gears, cadence and miles per hour to determine at what point you are most efficient. A good ratio for the novice on a 10 speed bicycle might be:

Front Chainwheels: 47 and 50 teeth

Rear Sprockets of Freewheel: 13, 15, 17, 19 and 22 teeth

This gives: *High Ratios:* 103.9, 97.6, 90

Middle Ratios: 84.6, 79.4, 74.6, 71.1

Low Ratios: 66.8, 61.4, 57.6

For those who do have an outmoded three or four speed hub gear, conversion derailleur sets can be added to update your cycling efficiency and performance, but this would need discussion with the local bicycle repair man. It might require a longer axle, new chain, wheel "re-dishing" (changing the hub's position in the wheel by tension adjustment of the spokes).

A special mention here about ratio combinations. Don't go overboard in demanding extreme combinations. Why?

A. Although the block has interchangeable sections, there are manufacturer limitations. B. A 15 speed gear needs a longer bottom bracket axle to handle the 3rd chainwheel. This puts the outside chainwheel even further right. If you try for odd or extreme combinations, you're asking the chain to assume an attitude of utmost angle, friction and tension. It's *not* efficient.

Quick Release Hubs: The quick-release hub is a luxury item to some folks. To me, it's a necessity. It's a time saver, finger-nail saver, and all-round nerve saver. It allows instant removal of the wheel without tools, which facilitates speedy disassembly for stashing the whole bicycle in the car, garage or storage area. It's especially appreciated if there's a puncture while cycling and the tire has to be removed. (Perish the thought!)

Basket(s): Baskets are advisable if you plan to grocery shop, but again I prefer loading the rear instead of the front. *Limited* groceries can be carried comfortably in the handlebar basket type carrier.

Pump: A necessity! Can be alloy or plastic, but never ride without it.

Lock: Cable type, locked by combination if you've got a good memory, key if you haven't!

The above items provide some insight into why some of those odd items that look like inquisition relics are really worthwhile. They add to those extra enjoyable minutes of coveted cycling time.

Bicycle Baskets

Front Basket

Rear Baskets

Pump

Lock

6

Adjusting the Bicycle and Cycling Technique

I've covered the basics of "what's needed," and if you live in a city where the bicycle you purchased has been adjusted by a well trained specialist you might skip this and go on to the next chapter. But again, you might pick up a few bits of information for future use. If your bicycle has just arrived by box, read on!

First, check for shipping damage. Axle nuts (if your bicycle does not have the quick release wheel hubs) should be on both front and rear wheels, and secured. If the hubs are quick release, the skewers (rods that go through the hubs) should have tension, but not be so tight that extreme pressure is required to open or close the release lever. Any minor adjustment can be made by a slight twist of the locking nut at the end of the skewer. It is seldom, if ever, that you would receive a new bicycle with this quick release mechanism not in perfect adjustment.

If the bicycle has tubular tires, make sure they are secured with sticky rim tape or rim cement. (This should come with the bicycle; however, 3M Brand Trim Adhesive can be substituted.) Anything else might set up a chemical reaction that will deteriorate the tubular.

If the tires are of the clincher type with inner tube separate from the casing, remove the wheel from the bicycle and put about 10 pounds of air in the tire. Bounce it like a ball, starting at the valve, for one complete revolution of the wheel. This prevents the tube, which might be caught in between the rim and outer casing, from being pinched and puncturing from rim friction.

To put air into either type of tire, check the sections on inflation of clincher tires and of tubular tires in Chapter 10.

After the tire is properly mounted install the wheel in the frame. Before locking either wheel in the frame, make sure it is correctly centered in the frame. For the rear wheel with its derailleur, drape the chain over the largest sprocket, insert the wheel into the seat stay ends, pull back until it's tight in the frame for correct tension, check to make sure it's centered properly, and *then* lock it in. Sounds complicated, but is routine after 2 or 3 tries.

Now to adjust the bicycle for comfort and efficiency. Any bicycle purchased must consider your own personal body design. This is true for children, as well as adults. The following four points have to be taken into consideration:

1. Length of leg from crotch to heel while standing in stocking feet.
2. Arm length from underarm to palm.
3. Height
4. Weight

A good rule of thumb: While straddling the diamond frame, there should be about an inch clearance from the top tube to the crotch. If there's more than an inch you need a larger frame size. If it's a tight fit or the pain causes your face to turn blue, you need a smaller frame or mixte frame. Fitting the bicycle goes hand-in-hand with the four statistics.

Once a correct frame size has been established the first adjustment is for saddle height. To obtain this, sit on the bicycle saddle, place the heel on the pedal. The leg should be straight without having to stretch or favor either side. If it isn't, adjust the height of the saddle accordingly. Then, when the foot is placed in proper position for cycling, the leg should have a slight bend at the knee when the foot reaches the bottom of the stroke.

To raise or lower the seat post tube and saddle, loosen the seat post bolt at the top of the seat tube. Apply pressure to raise or lower the seat. Tighten seat post bolt after correct positioning.

I might say here that it's wise to make sure it's tightened well. Nothing is worse than riding along and slowly your saddle and fanny sink down to the frame and your knees begin hitting your chin.

The saddle itself should be horizontal or with a very slight tip up, never down. A downward

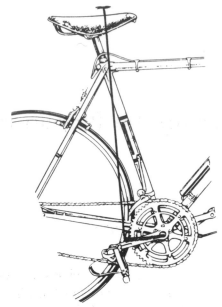

Saddle Positioning

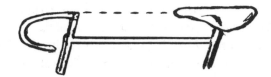

Saddle Angle and Handlebar Relationship

tipped saddle causes extra pressure on the arms and wrists from the body weight continually sliding forward on the saddle.

If the seat is too high, the rider will have to finish the stroke with the action of the toes. Not only is the full power of the leg lost, but extreme muscle cramps in the calf will develop. The actual "placing" of the saddle is negotiable. Generally your fulcrum body point should be approximately 8 or 9 inches back of the bottom bracket, regardless of the style of your saddle. Track racing cyclists like a more forward positioning of the saddle to aid in their initial power thrust.

I want to mention again that the sports or racing saddle will take a few weeks of riding before it feels comfortable. However, if its leather seems to be extremely hard after several hundred miles of cycling, treat it with a leather preserving oil or saddle soap. I have a dear friend who took a wooden mallet and lots of oil and pounded it for about three weeks. If you end up doing this, put a ladies shower cap or plastic

wrap over the saddle for a few weeks to keep your clothes from staining.

After adjusting the saddle for height and position, the next step is the handlebar. If you have extremely long arms, you may need to get a longer handlebar stem. I'm not in favor of moving the saddle back in extreme position to make up for long arms. To determine where the placement of your bar should be, start with the following:

A. Sit comfortable on the saddle and mark the saddle with chalk at the front of the crotch between your legs.
B. Measure arm length from underarm to mid-palm.
C. The distance from the crotch mark to where the top of the handlebar is to be placed should be approximately the same as the arm measurement length.

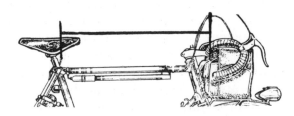

Handlebar Positioning

Example: If the distance from your underarm to palm is 24″, the distance from the crotch mark to the top of the bars should be 24″.

If you find the bar top is 2 or 3 inches further than your measurement, you need a shorter stem. If it's 2 or 3 inches shorter, you need a longer stem.

I'm not a rigid believer in fractions of inches making an extreme difference in comfort. I've ridden many bicycles, many times when a flat tire has necessitated borrowing a bicycle (in competition) and I've found as long as the frame fits and the basic good positioning has been established, the "fraction variables" are not important.

Make sure the handlebar top is at the approximate same height as the saddle. If it's too low, the rider suffers from excessive road shock in the wrists, arms and shoulders, from too much weight being transferred to the bar. If it's too high, the spinal area receives all the road shock, and the legs are kept from developing that lovely smooth, circular pedal action.

To raise or lower the handlebar, unscrew the expander bolt at the top of the stem to about 1/2 inch. Strike the bolt smartly with a hammer (don't pound) until it drops loose in the stem. Then move the stem up or down to the desired position. Tighten expander bolt after correct setting.

Good positioning should result in the equal distribution of body pressure to the three contact points, the bar, the saddle and the pedals. There isn't a better guide. It's aerodynamic and yet allows free breathing.

After you're satisfied with the positioning, use it for at least 200 to 300 miles. If something seems to give you a good bit of discomfort, correct the position; however, don't get involved in a weekly routine of trying something different.

Pedal Action: This is the most important phase of cycling to be *practiced* and learned. Specifically, it is the "flat-footed" technique, developed to get maximum power out of the thrust of the legs.

It CAN'T be done without toe-clips and straps, and since we're talking about efficient cycling, this point must be accepted by the novice.

I've talked about the pull-up action of the foot as being instrumental in developing this smooth

Foot Positioning for Efficient Cycling

rotational pedal action. Again, the necessity of owning a pair of cycling shoes and cleats is evident. They're not reserved for the racing cyclist, the touring rider needs them just as much to get that smooth cadence that prevents muscle cramp and spasm.

In order to develop this basic technique, the action of the flat-footed stroke has to be exaggerated. If I've screamed it once, I've screamed it one thousand times, "Drop your heels". . . . and that's just what you have to keep digesting over and over. I've even seen it taped on the top of a friend's bar.

With the rider beginning a stroke from the top position of the crank arm (twelve o'clock high), it's easy for the drop-heel action to be initiated. As the stroke continues around to 9 o'clock, the toes can be inclined with the heel still in the drop position.

However, when we get to the 6 o'clock position and the leg must now prepare to pull the crank up, the tendency is to raise the heel and pull back up with the toes. *Wrong, wrong, wrong!* It's at this point the drop heel technique has to be reinforced. The foot should be almost flat at the 3 o'clock return position, and in order to develop this, the dropped heel action has to receive constant concentration.

Take a test: *Try* rotating the cranks with the heel in an up position. The only power source is the toe and calf muscles.

Try rotating the cranks with the heel in a down position. The power source is the *whole leg*, and it's this power source that develops the smooth, rhythmic cadence that lets the tourist and racer put out "all they've got."

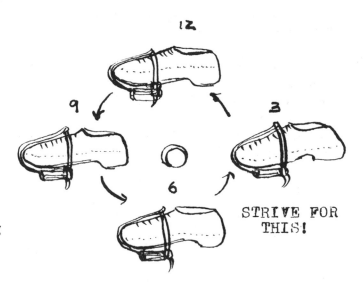

STRIVE FOR THIS!

7
Cycling Apparel

What to wear while cycling? If it's summer, any non-binding pants is good for either sex. Pedal pushers, bermudas, khaki's, slacks, most anything goes—Except short shorts. With short shorts, the large inner thigh muscles are exposed to rubbing against the saddle. If your legs are trim you might avoid the friction burn, but most novices would suffer.

However, I find the cycling shorts that are specially designed for bicycle riding are the best. They're lightweight wool or jersey that expand and retract with action. They have a wallet sized pocket that buttons, and a chamois lining for comfort. The chamois lining is really great, prevents friction burns and eliminates panties for women and athletic supporters for men. Why no undies? They have elastic waists that rub, sometimes elastic leg bands that rub, hems that bunch and chafe, and through the constant leg movement ALWAYS ride up under the shorts and begin to strangle your ever-tender posterior.

The only drawback is that they come in one color, black. Recently Simplicity Patterns called about good materials and styles for cycling shorts. This prompted me to visit my local dry-goods store. The variety of materials, stretchy man-made types is excellent. The purchase of a pattern, a chamois, elastic waist band, thread and material was under $4.00. With some slight alterations, I produced an attractive pants for 1/2 of what they retail at the cycle shops. They launder well with modern wash procedures and are good for years. I even wear them under my winter riding clothes.

Shirts of stretchy jersey or moisture absorbing stretchy materials are best. They should be the long torso type that can be worn over the shorts to prevent mid-back exposure. Nylon proves a problem (and so do some of the other synthetics) in that they don't absorb moisture for evaporation. When this happens you develop that cold, clammy feeling that can ruin your whole ride.

I personally don't like socks in the summer, but wear cotton footies. There's nothing worse than a suntan that ends above your ankle giving the effect of anemic feet. Looks dreadful when you're dressed.

Cycling gloves are an add or subtract item. They're great in the summer when the bar seems to make the hands sticky, and vice-versa, but then again, you end up with anemic looking hands.

On cool, nippy days, I add a track suit designed for cycling, but any of the non-binding slacks and windbreaker-jackets are excellent. I'm not adverse to thermal long-johns underclothing either. Mittens with long cuffs are great and scarves and ear warmers provide the finishing touch. Any all-head covering seems to create too much body heat and perspiration.

In the winter, when it's cold but well above freezing, I add wool socks and occasionally large size plastic baggies that fit over the whole foot. This keeps the air from penetrating the shoe. Feet are the first, and really only part of the body to get cold. For the avid cold weather cyclist, there are socks that have heating filaments in their weaving and with a battery operated contact keep the feet warm for hours.

Cycling shoes are an absolute necessity. They have a steel arch that keeps the thrust of the foot from bending the shoe and wasting effort and energy. They're also designed to accommodate the shoe bottom cleat that fits into the pedal and keeps the shoe from slipping back out of the pedal and toe clip during the pull-up motion. The best way to break in the shoe for the cleat is to use the shoe two or three times until a good pedal indentation is established in the shoe sole. Then have your shoemaker nail on the cleat so that the slip opening is exactly where the pedal indentation shows.

Rain capes are available if you're going to tour; however, I have to explain a major difficulty encountered with a rain cape. It's water tight, so it's air tight . . . and because it's air tight the rider begins to perspire. Very shortly you're as wet under from perspiration as from the outside downpour, and probably smelling pretty ripe. But if it's cold and raining, it's probably best to don the rain cape anyway.

Pedal Indentation on Shoe; Cleat Placement

8

Programming for Everyday Cycling

Now that I've discussed some of the "what's needed," let's get down to the "how to." First, let me say I know what it means to make time for a fitness training program. And now, after five children I have to plan to find time for recreational cycling.

Now I *really* appreciate what I learned during my racing career. Not points in stamina, sprinting, technique and strategy, but how to get the most enjoyable, beneficial cycling out of the precious jaunts I now manage.

I don't speak just for women; the problem of obtaining the most in enjoyable cycling is the same for both sexes. And the desires are the same: exercise, physical fitness, a trim figure, and an enjoyable time.

Secondly, an applied program is not just once a week. It's sitting down, looking over your time and saying to yourself: "Four times this week and every week, I will spend 45 minutes enjoying the great outdoors and keeping fit!" Then you'll fit the time into your busy schedule before committing that precious time to other outside activities. Remember, if you're dead from a cholesterol overload you wouldn't be able to attend the activity anyway. After the first month of programming, you most likely will want to up the time from 45 minutes to that hour and 15 minute ride.

Now, the "nitty-gritty." I have to emphasize a very important fact about using your bicycle program as a physical fitness media. If you intend to use it for this purpose and not just a daily sight-seeing jaunt, expect to become perspired. I see ad after ad on the television showing lithe-figured girls with gorgeous hair-do's daintily manipulating horrendous contraptions in the local gymnasium. Now, this is out and out fraud! If you really expect your fitness program to reduce those bulges and flatten that gut you have to work at it and burn up those calories. Almost every calorie chart lists the amount needed for each individual work type. Most of us need barely 1,500 per day. In order to burn up those extra goodies we sneak in, you have to (and I can't say it in dainty terms) work up a stinking sweat. That's why the clothing has to be absorbent. That's why the time you choose to exercise should fit into your program so you don't find yourself exercising right before a dinner date, or after visiting the beauty salon.

Unless you cycle with your husband when he arrives home, a good time for the average housewife to plan her riding is between 12 and 2 in the afternoon. The house has been straightened, children are at school, there's time for a shower, hair-set and meal preparation before the family attacks the house again. For myself, I do both. I back-pack my two year old in my Gerry Carrier and go in the afternoons, or go with my husband after work with the whole family.

Single girls seem to find their best time to cycle right after work. There's time for a shower after the ride before any dinner date.

And now, an extra hint for homemakers—because it's directed toward that handsome wage-earner who keeps you both well fed and fully clothed. When he walks in the door after work, have his bicycle tires pumped, his shorts and shoes draped on the frame, and a glass of "Gatorade" in your hand. It's a part of wifely duties to

Back Packing Holly—Courtesy Paul Gach

reduce the number of things he has to prepare before you both go for your ride. If you can lug a 30 pound toddler around, you can surely carry a non-squirming 30 pound bicycle. And pumping tires is additional good exercise for the stomach and arm muscles! Don't defeat him with "Honey, will you—blah-blah-blah for me? *Do it for him. A husband is like good champagne—carefully preserved, he improves with age!*

Very important for beginners: Don't ask friends to accompany you unless they have similar equipment. Nothing is more defeating to two people than one who is properly equipped and has to continually slow down to let the red faced, blue fingered, panting companion catch up. It's unbelievably frustrating and the very fast end of a very long friendship.

If you and your husband plan to cycle together with other beginners, get together first with your equipment. Become familiar with the bicycle. Practice taking off and putting back both rear

and front wheels. Get on the bicycle and try the brakes. A slight finger pressure on the levers is all that's needed to slow the bicycle. At a good speed it's easier to brake by the pumping method of apply pressure, release, apply pressure, release. (Car racing drivers borrowed this from us cyclists!)

The Everyday Anklers—Courtesy John Mitchell

Practice shifting gears, inserting feet into toe clips and straps, stopping and removing the feet from the toe clips and straps—without falling.

Once you're familiar with the bicycle, get organized for that first ride. Bear in mind that any sport in which you participate for the first time will result in muscular strain if you "over-do." It will most likely result in some aches and pains anyway. However, these disappear quickly if a sound and sensible schedule is maintained.

Keep your first rides down to about 8 or 10 miles. Now this sounds like a lot, but you'll be doing this in your 45 to 60 minute ride, and the tendency of the beginner seems to be "Gosh, that's not enough, I'll just continue my ride." Don't! Try a week or two of using time as a guide and keep it under an hour each time.

Find an area where you're not forced to brake and stop at every corner. Plaza parking areas are great for this during off hours. Many states have cycle paths, bikeways and other marked bike routes. Many automobile associations can give you a map listing scarcely travelled roads.

When you begin your first ride, cycle at a pace that is warming but not hard. Don't wait until you're fatigued to get off the cycle. Try riding for 20 minutes, get off and walk for 5 minutes, get back on the bicycle and finish your final 20 minutes. Don't sit down during this 5 minute break; the walk is refreshing in itself.

Chat Time—Courtesy John Mitchell

Touring groups that travel from 40 to 80 miles a day use this technique. When I've led groups (seasoned riders as well as beginners) 5 minutes out of every hour cycled is spent walking. It's always refreshing and gives time for a chat about any problems that may have come up.

If you're planning to do some night riding, I would recommend one of the lightweight generator sets that gets its power from tire contact, or the removable headlamp-flashlight that can be used off the bicycle. There are even arm-band lights powered by battery that are excellent. In addition to the headlight, make sure you have a tail-light attachment to the generator, a very large reflector, and wear special reflecting clothes or illuminated safety strips. At the speed cars travel, even a beacon might not be enough to protect the cyclist.

Since you occasionally will find yourself bothered by man's best friend with voracious teeth, you might invest in one of the pepper derivative aerosol sprays that the mailman uses. One good shot is usually enough to set up a memory bank reaction in the dog that will forestall future attacks. It's also a lot less expensive than replacing torn clothing or pumps that have been bent into the shape of a dog's head. Immediately discount any old-wives tales that a barking dog never bites.

Carry a cable lock that can be wound through the bicycle frame and to a solid object. There's too much money invested in a bicycle to be careless.

Refreshments? On a short ride of an hour or an hour and a half, you normally wouldn't need any refreshment. But if you want something, I recommend the purchase of a bicycle bottle and carrier . . . and ultimately that great stuff "Gatorade," or products of this type. Plain, ordinary water should be sufficient in most cases.

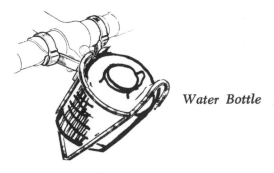

Water Bottle

A small warning when out with your bicycle and you have stopped and parked: before remounting, always pick up the rear of the bicycle and push the pedal around for one complete revolution. Many times curious children (and lame-brained adults) have come by and pushed the gear shifting levers. This moves the gear mechanism into a different position, but leaves the chain still in the old position. By spinning the crank arm, it would rotate the rear wheel and automatically drop the chain into the position the gear lever had selected (taking care of the chainwheel shifter at the same time). Technically, starting off with the lever out of position won't hurt the derailleur, but the initial hard power thrust used to propel the bicycle forward makes an excessive strain on the chain while it's busy getting itself back to where it should be.

I might say here, that any major repairs of derailleurs should be handled by a cycle shop—or for that matter, *any* major repairs. I still have a loose bearing in my bicycle tubing that rattles every time I pick up the bicycle. The clickity-clickity-clack is my constant reminder to forget about a complete overhaul on the "do it yourself" basis. Most bicycle shops charge an approximate $30.00 overhaul fee, but it's complete, and covers every part of the bicycle.

Let's face reality: repairing any item with which you are not familiar is impossible. Listing explicit instructions in repairs is only one-half the battle. Functional ability to attempt these repairs requires that "feeling" for correct adjustment, tension, as well as the tools that the specialized bicycle needs. For all my experience, I cannot tell the correct tension for my track wheels from that of my road wheels and when I've replaced spokes, I always have the wheel "trued."

9

Bicycle Maintenance

There are some things that the average "tinkerer" can do to keep the bicycle in marvelous condition until time for that annual check-up. Although many don't bother, the best *method* is to do it *methodically,* cleaning a little each day—handlebars and brakes on one day, rims and hubs another, etc. In this way, the machine never really gets dirty and the constant upkeep adds life to the bicycle.

If you do get caught in wet weather, be sure to wipe the machine dry immediately. I also recommend going over the metal parts with a clean cloth saturated with oil.

Here's a basic list that can be handled by most of us. And again, I think the wife should be responsible for keeping "hubby's" bicycle clean. If he's responsible for the car, you should be responsible for his bicycle!

Adjust every month: —All nuts to be sure they're tight.

Oil every month: —All bearing surfaces (places that have ball bearings)

—Brake levers, brake joints. (Keep oil off of the rubber lever hoods.)

—All external moving parts or surfaces

—Pedals

—Chains

The Army has an old saying, "If it can't salute or move, paint it." When it comes to bicycles, "If it moves, oil it once a month."

Tools for this trade should be:

—Adjustable crescent wrench

—Screw Driver

—Pliers

For those who like a more comprehensive check-list, use the following with reference to the Parts Chart:

1. Wheel Hubs: wipe clean and oil at bearing surfaces. Wheels should spin freely.
2. Rims and Spokes: wipe clean with oil-saturated cloth. Spokes should be tight and wheel rim round. If you develop loose spokes they can be tightened with a spoke wrench. But if the wheel gets out of "true" (not round), it has to be tightened professionally.
3. Sports Brake: oil front and rear brake joints. Brake cables should be oiled so they move freely in their housings (coverings). Also, check to see all cable housings curve gradually. Eliminate any sharp kinks or bends. Replace worn or frayed cables and housings. Check to make sure brake blocks are secured tightly to brake arms.
4. Sports Gear—Hub Type: be sure it shifts smoothly. If not, have the bicycle repairman show you how to adjust it. Oil hub gear changer lever and keep cable oiled and friction free.

   Sports-Gear—Derailleur Type: wipe cage with clean oil saturated cloth to remove grime. Oil all moving parts of mechanism, levers, cables leading to gear. If you develop difficulty with the derailleur, it must be adjusted by the bicycle repair man.
5. Sprockets and Chainwheels: wipe sprocket or sprocket block with clean oiled cloth. Oil sprocket block at bearing surface. Wipe chainwheels with clean oiled cloth. Make certain all pins that hold the chainwheel to the crank are secured.

6. Bottom Bracket and Crank Assembly: wipe all parts with clean oiled cloth. Any adjustment of bracket has to be made by repairman. Check to make sure the crank's cotter pins (pinning devices that attach cranks to axle) are secured.

7. Pedals, Toe Clips and Straps: oil pedal bearing surfaces, keep wiped clean. Check to be sure toe clips are tightly secured to pedals. Check straps for damage and replacement.

8. Chain: wipe clean and keep well oiled. Occasionally remove and soak chain in kerosene, brush with stiff wire brush, oil and replace chain. (Derailleur chain must be removed with chain link extractor tool. All other chains can usually be removed by release of the connecting master link.) Chains eventually stretch with normal wear and need to be replaced about every 1,500 miles or sooner if the chain shows wear.

9. Brake Levers: tighten locking nuts on levers to keep them from moving on the handlebar. Be sure to oil lever pivot points, but be careful to keep oil from getting on the lever's rubber hoods.

10. Front Fork: oil both top and bottom bearing surfaces, wipe clean at both places.

11. Stem: check to be certain stem is locked tightly into head tube.

12. Handlebar: if your handlebar is separate from the stem, make certain the bar is locked tightly into the stem.

13. Saddle: check to be sure positioning bolts under saddle are secured. Be sure seat post holding saddle is secured into seat tube.

14. Warning Device: if velvet throated, have a bell or horn and be sure it works.

15. Reflector or Tail Light: check to make sure it is secured. Either should be visible from at least 300 feet.

16. Headlight: check to make sure it is secured and alive. If it's the generator type, be sure the activating arm correctly meets the side of the tire.

17. Front and rear Carriers: if they are not the brazed on type, constantly check to see if they remain secured to the bicycle frame.

18. Inflation of Tires: check for correct tire pressure listed in chart. Tubular tires should be filled before riding and have their air released after the ride is completed. Otherwise, constant air pressure causes stitching to give and the tire will blow. For further detail, read the separate chapter on Tires.

19. Last, but not least, keep the bicycle *hung* when you're not riding. It's out of the way where small-fry can't get at it, and tires are protected from rim cuts. A large hook is great for this, can be put in basement ceiling or garage. Bicycles can be hung by either rear or front wheel.

10
Tires—The Critical Item

I have to devote a whole chapter to tires. They're the one critical item on the bicycle that sooner or later will give someone trouble. To begin with,

Roadside Repair—Courtesy Detroit Council A.Y.H.

make sure you know exactly how much air pressure your tires must have. Underinflation is as bad as overinflation. Also consider outside temperatures. If it's hot outside and pressures build it's better to underinflate a little. If it's cool a few extra pounds can be tempered. Most tires carry air pressure regulations on the side.

Weight of Rider		125 lb.	150 lb.	175 lb.	200 lb.
Clincher Touring Tires	26 x 1¼″	45	55	60	65
(650 B)	26 x 1⅜″	45	50	55	60
	26 x 1½″	40	45	50	55
	26 x 1¾″	35	40	45	50
Clincher Racing Tires	27 x 1¼″	65	70	75	80
Tubular Touring Tires	27 x 1¼″	70	75	80	85
Tubular Road Racing		80	85	95	100
Tubular Track Racing		95	95	105	115

Because of the weight proportion on the rear wheel, the front tire can carry approximately 5 pounds less than specified.

Tires come with many different tread styles, weight and design. Pick and choose what you think best suits your needs. There are only a few basic "no-no's."

1. Don't try to ride the ultra-light track racing tires on the road.
2. Don't expect the "gravel grinder" to give much performance on the track.

Inflation of the Clincher Tire: This can be done with the bicycle hand pump and lots of energy, or the local gas station air compressor. Although many gas stations have a metered air compressor that can be pre-set for the correct air pressure, it's wise to invest in an air gauge to prevent over-inflation.

To inflate the clincher tire by either hand pump or compressor, you need only firmly apply the air hose connection to the tube's Schraeder valve.

Schraeder Valve

Then, pump away—or if you're at one of those lovely gas station meters, let the compressor do it.

Inflation of the Tubular Tire: Again, this can be done with the bicycle hand pump or the local gas station air compressor. There are a few differences.

To inflate the tubular tire with the small Presta

Presta Valve

valve, first unscrew the small sealing knob at the top of the valve. Tap it with your finger to make sure it's free. Then if you're using the bicycle hand pump, merely screw the pump connector directly on to the opened valve and pump away.

However, if you intend to use the gas station compressor you'll need a valve adapter. One

Valve Adapter

should come with your new bicycle, or they can be purchased at any lightweight bicycle shop.

Screw on the valve adapter to the opened valve and then apply the compressor connection. To close valve after tire is inflated, just retighten the sealing knob at the top of the valve. Replace the adapter on the closed valve to make sure it's not misplaced.

Remember to release the air from your tubular tires after your ride. Also, check all tires for imbedded stones, foreign objects or other sticky muck. Wipe clean with a damp cloth. A small stiff brush helps remove most debris.

Spare tires should be mounted on a separate rim or wheel, inflated to the point where they are firm and then stored in a dry, airy place.

Now, what to do when you hear that horrible "pppsssssss," clunk, clunk, clunk (valve making contact with cement). *Naturally,* you carry either a spare tube for your clincher tire, or a spare tubular. So you just remove the wheel from the frame, change the tire and set aside 15 minutes or so that night for repairs.

Let's start with the clincher tire: If you have a flat and there is no visible evidence of a puncture or leak, begin by removing the wheel from the bicycle. Lay the wheel flat. There are three little tools called tire irons that you must have.

Take one iron and wedge the blunted end between the rim edge under the tire's top bead (edge). Hook the other slotted side around a spoke. This automatically pops the tire edge above the rim.

Tire Irons

Clincher Tire Removal

Place the second tool three or four spokes away, in the same manner. Then, take the third tool and carefully insert it under a loose spot past the second tool. In this position, pull it all around the rim back to the first inserted tool. This releases the tire from the rim.

Next, push the tube valve back through the rim valve hole and gently remove the inner tube from the tire. Pump some air into the tube and submerge it 12 to 14 inches at a time until you've discovered the leak.

If it's a minute hole, you might have to pump extra air into the tube before you spot it. Once the hole is discovered, mark it and deflate the tube.

Patch according to the instructions on your repair kit. Usually:

1. Rough the spot on the tube where the hole appears.
2. Apply cement. *Let cement dry*
3. Apply rubber patch and press firmly over cemented area.

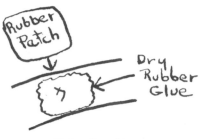

Tube Patching

After the hole is patched, check your tire to see if there is any foreign object imbedded in the tire at the point where the tube leaked. If so, remove it.

If you have a good cut in the tire, I suggest glueing a patch over that hole inside the tire, in the same manner the tube was patched. You can also glue a cut section from an old clincher as reinforcement if it's really a big slash. However, this produces a bump, bump effect while riding if it's a large piece.

After checking the tire to be sure you've repaired all the damaged areas, replace the tube inside the tire, making sure the valve is in the valve hole. Force the tire bead back inside the rim with the blunt end of the rim tool.

When the tire is secured, put 5 to 10 pounds of air into the tube. Bounce the wheel like a ball, one complete revolution of the wheel, to make sure the tube is not caught between the rim and tire bead. Then inflate to correct air pressure and replace on bicycle.

For Tubular Tires: Remove the wheel from the bicycle. To remove the tire from the rim, press firmly on a part of the tire opposite from the valve hole. Keep applying pressure until the tire slides off the rim. It's hard on fingers, but tools can't be used.

Carefully pull the tire loose to the valve hole and then push the valve back through the hole and remove the tire.

If you can see the puncture spot, fine, but due to the nature of this tire's construction (the tube sewn into the casing and then a protective gummed tape cemented over the sewing) a minute hole is hard to find. If the puncture is not immediately discernable, mount the tire on a rim.

Then, fill a pan with water, inflate to 60 or 70 pounds of air and start at the valve to rotate the tire slowly in the water. Invariably air bubbles will appear at the base of the valve stem, as this is the only sizeable opening in the casing. However, continue to rotate the tire until you find the spot on the tire that shows another seepage of air.

Mark it well with a crayon and dry the tire with a clean cloth.

With a thin, but not sharp tool (I use a screw driver), raise about five inches of the tape that covers the sewing. With scissors cut the thread about 2 1/2 inches on each side of the puncture. Don't dig down to cut the threads; you might ruin the tube. Just sever at the top. Remove the cut threads with tweezers.

Open the casing and gently pull up about six inches of tube. Inflate tube gently with a hand pump to locate the air hole if it's not visible. Once you've found the hole, mark it.

Let the air out of the tube. Place your pump under the tube so the area on which you are working is flat without wrinkles.

Scrape the whole hole area with an emery paper (Fingernail boards are fine, too.) Apply light film of rubber cement. After it has dried, (without your blowing on it) apply the finest grade of tire patch.

You might want to put a small patch on the inside of the tire itself, as well.

Very important: Check for leaks in the same general area. Nothing is as maddening as completing the whole operation and then finding there's another hole in the same area.

Before replacing the tube back in the tire, sprinkle the inside with cornstarch or dust from one of those commercial chalk containers that come with the repair kit. (I even used Johnson's Baby Powder in an emergency.) This prevents the tube from sticking to the tire casing.

Again, if there's a big slit in the tire, you have to reinforce this perforation with a two or three inch piece of casing, or the pressured tube will be forced right out the slit.

Return the tube back into the casing, being extremely careful to see that the tube seats itself well in the tire, and not near the edge where you'll be sewing.

Then to sew! Use the special three cornered

needle for this job. This, and the best quality special thread can be obtained at your local cycle shop. However, most department stores carry a curved, three-cornered glovers needle, and high test fishing line that can duplicate for the sewing thread.

Start your stitches two or three back over the good stitches. Lay end threads over the area to be sewn (use thread double) so they will automatically be locked in as you stitch over them. This saves making knots that might work into the casing and cause friction.

Match the holes together and use a plain over-

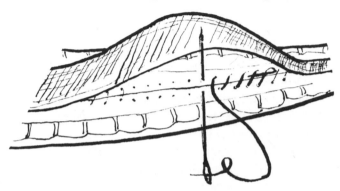

Tubular Tire Repair

hand stitch. Sew firmly in the same manner of the original tension. Finish by sewing 2 stitches over the old sewing and pulling thread under the last loop several times to lock it.

Apply rubber cement over the stitches and on the underside of your loosened tire tape. Allow both to dry and then press tire tape back down on top of sewn stitches to its original place.

Remount the tire on the wheel by inserting the valve through the rim valve hole and then easing the tire on around the rim with both hands. If you discover that the sticky tape that holds the tire to the rim is dry, you might need to replace this first and then remount the tire. If you have

used rim cement and find this has dried up, it will have to be roughed and scraped and a new coat applied. Directions come with the mastics.

Inflate the tire hard so that the tape and tire will be under normal riding pressure. Deflate after 3 or 4 hours.

Tires ridden on a bicycle velodrome require extreme care in seeing that the tire is firmly attached to the rim. And if shellac is used it has to be applied in separate coats (3 or 4) letting each dry, and then mounting the tire with the last coat slightly tacky. If you're a beginner, ask a seasoned cyclist to show you how.

Helpful hints: Aside from punctures which are inevitable, the majority of tubular blow-outs are caused by separated stitching from overinflation. *Always* deflate tires about 50% after a ride. Naturally they have to be reinflated before another ride, but it's cheaper than buying new tires every month.

You can spot a stitching break before it blows and prevent the blow by reinforcing the stitching. How to spot the break? The tire bulges out rather pregnantly on both sides of the loosened stitching. If you're on the road when this develops (you'll feel a thump-thump, as that spot comes in contact with the pavement), stop immediately and deflate the tire to where there's enough air in it so it appears normal. Then wind tape (any sticky kind) around both tire and rim at this weakened spot. Reinflate the tire to where it's rideable (about 3/4 of capacity pressure) *Remembering not to apply the caliper brake to that wheel,* and finish the ride. If you're stuck for tape, you can unwind your handlebar tape and use that.

After the ride, repair the stitching as necessary, remembering to go about an extra 1/2 inch on each side of the stitching break to reinforce that already weakened thread.

11

Cycling Rules and Regulations

There are actually very few traffic rules that differ in car driving or bike riding. I suggest you check first with your local police department to determine if there are any extra ordinances that apply to cycling in your area.

It might be surprising to learn there are a few you never knew existed. For instance, in my city, children under 12 are not permitted to ride in the street. Children from 12 to 16 are allowed *only* if they have the written permission of their parent in their pocket! I'm willing to wager very few parents are aware of this ordinance, and yet it's a common one in the big cities.

And for heaven's sake, buy a license. If your bicycle is stolen (it's seldom lost) the police turn a very deaf ear toward locating a bicycle that the owner was unwilling to license for 50¢.

When a bicycle is stolen, it's generally ridden and dropped by some smart-assed kid in a nearby field, (nearby to where he lives, of course)! Or else, it's stolen by the professionals who remove most of the equipment and dump the frame in an alley or field.

When the bicycle is licensed, it carries the serial number stamped on the frame and can be returned, and it's a lot less expensive to re-equip a bicycle than buy the whole bicycle again. Another important fact is that many insurance companies will cover such losses.

General Rules: Observe all traffic regulations—
    Red and Green Lights!
    Stop Signs!
    One-Way Streets!

It's embarrassing for a 38 year old mother of five to appear in traffic court to explain her own traffic violation with five pairs of very smug, sparkling eyes smiling up at the judge.

1. Don't weave in and out of slow-moving traffic. Drivers seldom realize that the sports cycle is travelling between 15 and 20 m.p.h.
2. Keep to the right of the road. *Never ride against traffic.*
3. Yield the right of way to pedestrians. Learn that children can't be trusted to move in any obvious direction.
4. Ride single file unless it's an organized group and then two abreast is the limit.
5. One on a bike unless it's a tandem.
6. Keep both hands on the handlebars except when signaling a turn. Always signal a right turn with the left arm extended in an upward position.
   A left turn should be handled by crossing the intersection, waiting for the light to change and then starting off in the new direction.
7. Have a bell or buzzer for a warning device if you're velvet throated. In some countries a warning device is mandatory.
8. Watch out for cars pulling out into traffic from the curb, or the sudden opening of automobile doors. Auto doors are one of the greatest causes of cycling accidents, and very hard on the bicycle repair bill.
9. Keep well back from slow moving cars; they may stop suddenly or turn directly in front of you. Very few drivers realize that cyclists can easily sustain the 20 m.p.h. of slow moving traffic.
10. Be alert for pedestrians who step from between parked cars.

11. Avoid the urge to see how fast you can go downhill. That's just the time the student driver decides to pull out of a side street because he *knows* bicycles can only go 3 or 4 m.p.h.

12. If you're riding after dark, wear some approved reflecting material, as well as using your head and tail lights. However, it's my "rule of thumb" that one just doesn't ride after dark. There is just too much traffic, moving too swiftly.

13. If you want to use the bicycle for local shopping, have appropriate baskets or saddle bags. Don't try and steer with one hand and carry eggs in the other: bicycle omelette.

14. A word about radios. *No.* I can't imagine anyone going out to enjoy a bicycle ride with a radio glued to the ear. It's distracting and dangerous.

15. If you're involved in any type of accident, make sure there is a police involvement to protect you from legal action.

16. Remember, everyone out on the road except you is a ridiculous drunken idiot without driving experience or concept of danger.

An amazing thing will happen as you cycle. Your car driving awareness will improve with what you have discovered while cycling.

12

Winter and Indoor Cycling

What to do when the temperature falls below freezing? Well, there are those who keep riding. But it's not pleasant under any circumstances. The nose runs, the eyes water, the cheeks become frost bitten and it's really impossible to have an enjoyable ride.

The answer to this problem for me came through the initial investment I made in my cycling equipment, and you might want to invest as I did, but there's a less expensive apparatus that is just as efficient.

A. Rollers: relatively expensive

B. Cycle-cisor Conversion Kit: inexpensive

Hearty Winter Cyclers—Courtesy Baranet

Rollers

A. *Rollers:* Every racing cyclist sooner or later has to have a portable roller outfit that will be used for winter training, or warm-ups before racing. How to ride them? Place the rear wheel of your bicycle on the twin rollers and the front wheel on the single roller. Use a box to mount the bicycle and have one hand free to support yourself upright (near a wall is an excellent place to begin). Start to pedal. Centrifugal force will keep the bicycle upright and your smooth pedalling will keep it steady and on the rollers. There's no need to steer, just rest the hands on the top of the bar naturally. Visually concentrate on a spot

two or three feet in front of the wheel, to keep from overcontrolling the steering.

For a beginner, it's wise to have someone hold the rider by the rear of the saddle, just for security. After you've ridden two or three times, your own confidence will let you handle it.

B. *Cycle-cisor Conversion Kit:* With this unit you can attach your own bicycle to the apparatus (rear wheel only), mount the bicycle and pedal away. Although it's not recommended for bicycles with derailleur gears, I have hooked up one for a friend with the limitation that he can't change gears while using the kit. A caution here: The trend is to always tighten the tension wheel that rides against

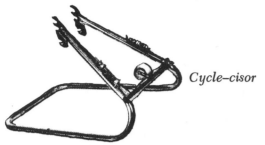

Cycle–cisor

the rear tire to the point where it's difficult and exhausting to pedal. This completely defeats the purpose in cycle exercising. Just maintain a slight friction point so that the action of pedalling can be completed just like that of riding on the road. No pile driving, just a smooth circular cadence.

What gear to ride? Since there is so little friction or resistance for either indoor contraption, I recommend starting in the high 80's and going up to the limit that racers use in roller racing, 96.

How long? Start with three minutes a day, attempting to keep the r.p.m.'s between 80 and 90. When you can do the three minutes at 100 r.p.m.'s, go up again in the gear ratios and add another two minutes.

It should take about 6 or 8 weeks to get to about 100 r.p.m.'s for a 10 minute stretch. Then if you're really trying to develop the lung's capacity, sprint (go as fast as you can for an additional 30 seconds to a minute.) I can guarantee the perspiration will be rolling off the nose, arms, back and chest.

As a homemaker, I can't make it out on the road every day even in the summer. So I've developed and improvised what I call Baranet's Basic Bulge Battle. I take my rollers and bicycle outside, don my bikini, and in the privacy of our yard peddle for about 15 minutes in the warm sun. Great for tanning and exercising at the same time.

Sun and Cycling—Courtesy Paul Gach

13
Touring by Bicycle

Touring by bicycle is the best way known to really see things—and it's not just seeing, it's hearing, smelling and feeling, too.

When you hike-tour it's slow and you can't cover much territory unless you thumb your way along.

When you car tour, it's bumper to bumper at 75 m.p.h. until you get to the destination and then you're generally limited to points of interest at this spot. How many times have you been driving and spotted something the whole family would like to investigate, only to find it was fifteen miles before the next exit?

And really, there's nothing to compare to the fresh, cool breezes, the songs of woodland birds, the chatter of crows and squirrels, the put-put-put of partridge, the smell of mock orange, cedar and pine as you quietly pedal through seldom travelled backlands.

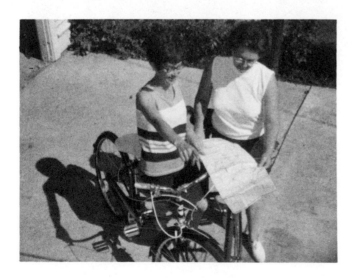

How to get the most out of your one day touring jaunts? Plan ahead! First, get a map of your local area and a pencil compass. Then draw a 30 to 40 mile radius using your area as home base. Within that circle there will be points of interest that you never dreamed could be reached without a car or a great deal of effort—and they're all waiting!

Many will not be at the point where it would require the total of 80 miles (40 out and 40 back), but only 10 or 15 miles away, requiring a round trip of only 20 or 30 miles.

The second procedure is to decide your goal for the day. Do you want a long cycling and seeing round trip, or a shorter cycle-stop-browse adventure?

If you're an adult cyclist (over 18 in my life style) try and ride with a touring group before you begin your own planning. Cycle paths that offer specific protected mileage for both bicycle and rider are marvelous. There have been so many cycle paths developed in the last three years that the only nearly complete and up-to-date listings can be obtained from:

Bicycle Institute of America—Attention: Cycle Paths
122 E. 42nd Street
New York, N.Y., 10017

One day hostelling trips are a wonderful adventure and can educate the beginner in the basic touring fundamentals. For local hostel office write:

Early Planning—Courtesy Jessie Miley

Group Assembly—Courtesy Detroit Council A.Y.H.

American Youth Hostels
20 West 17th Street
New York, N.Y., 10017

Other sources of touring companionship can be made through:

League of American Wheelmen—Attention: Mrs. J. L. Hart
5118 Foster Avenue
Chicago, Illinois, 60630

Bicycle Touring League of America—Attention: Roland C. Geist
260 W. 260th Street
New York, N.Y., 10471

International Bicycle Touring Society—Attention: Dr. Clifford Graves

846 Prospect Street
La Jolla, California, 92037

Many racing clubs have a touring contingency. Write to:

Amateur Bicycle League of America—Attention: Ernest Seubert
137 Brunswick Road
Cedar Grove, N.J. 07009

And for a special situation, you might want to advertise in:

Bicycle News,
12 Cherry St.
Brattleboro, Vt. 05301

Even advertising in your local paper is a great means of "getting together." I tried this in Dear-

A.Y.H. 4th of July Parade Group—Courtesy Detroit Council A.Y.H.

born several years ago, and over 150 people arrived. . . . from 9 years to 57!

There are many annual touring classic events where hundreds and even thousands participate, and these are really marvelous experiences. Call your local newspaper's sports editor and he would most likely know about anything within 100 miles of your area.

One of the biggest is the TOSRV (Tour of Scioto River Valley) a 210 mile, 2 day, round trip from Columbus, Ohio to Portsmouth, Ohio under the direction of the Columbus American Youth Hostels.

Another is a Bicycle Marathon at Belle Isle, Detroit, Michigan, where cyclists can ride as much as they want during the 48 hour period. Write direct to Detroit Department of Parks and Recreation.

Any of these big events handle all accommodations. . . . sleeping, eating, comfort stations, first aid, repair stations, for a *really* nominal charge.

But if you live in "backwoodsville" and there aren't bicycle paths, or organized cycling associations available and you plan to do it yourself . . . here are some helpful hints:

1. Where to go? Everywhere! When to go? As long as it's not too cold. Begin the spring season with rides for morel mushrooms, wildflowers, strawberries and raspberries. The summer's great for rides to lakes, swim parties, picnics, fresh fruit stands loaded with all sorts of mouth watering oral satisfiers. Anytime is great if you're an avid rock collector, antique fancier, or bird watcher. The fall is surely

TOSRV Columbus, Ohio—Courtesy Columbus Council A.Y.H.

nature's most colorful season, and cycling trips to wooded areas with sketch pad, painting knives, brushes and small canvasses give cycling the final touch of combining physical exercise, nature and the arts. And don't forget the cider and donut rides. I'd recommend going light on the cider if it's a long trip back. Over-indulgence is the key to consistent, continual, emergency potty-stops.

2. Check out the planned route by car first, or on clearly defined maps. Make sure it has some access to communities so if an emergency situation arises you're able to be reached. This works both ways. If some family member wishes to contact you, it can be handled easily. Or if you end up in a bloody mess after a non-negotiable road hole, you'll be found before your bones rot.

3. The majority of information about actual riding techniques has been covered in Chapter 8. Be sure you've absorbed all you can.

4. Know the exact mileage you'll be covering. An additional ten mile oversight might be the crushing blow to you, or some other member of the group, or even the whole group. Can you imagine six other people with bicycles trying to flag down a cab to take them home?

5. Start early. I always liked 7:30 a.m. This gave 2 1/2 hours of cycling, an hour or 2 to browse and 2 1/2 hours return . . . and generally brought the group back by 3:30 or 4:00,

Detroit Bicycle Marathon—Courtesy Bill Olsen

Cherry Pickin'—Courtesy Jessie Miley

Road resting—Courtesy Detroit Council A.Y.H.

A day's planned tour—Courtesy Detroit Council A.Y.H.

Roadside Self–Service–Courtesy Pat Mitchell

carried a thermos full of hot soup (or cold martinis)! It's so much more refreshing to find a lovely wooded brook-side spot than one of those stiff air-conditioned, four walled food palaces whose bill of fare will be the approximate replacement cost of four new tires.

9. In connection with the above, consider the fruits and vegetables in season if you'll be cycling into farmland. There's little tastier than home grown goodies that can be purchased right out of the fields from roadside stands. It always gives one a sense of self-satisfaction to have removed the "middleman's" profit.

missing most of the weekend traffic. Again, remember to walk at least five minutes out of every hour.

6. Wear comfortable, attractive clothing (Discussed in Chapter 7). In addition to what I've written, I'd like to say there's no need to down-grade cycling by riding in dirty threadbare potato sacks that have the appearance of one who has been ravished and raped. This applies to both sexes! The cycling tights or stretchy shorts, attractive jerseys, etc. should be clean and well mended. Sun glasses, cycling shoes and gloves, all help make up the well-dressed cyclist. A single saddle-bag that fits under the saddle can accommodate additional long pants, windbreakers or raincoat for that extreme weather change.

7. By all means, carry a spare tube and changing tools or tire. These fit easily into the saddle bag.

8. If you want to carry a water bottle and pack some sandwiches, I'm all for that! I've even

Cycling Saddlemen–Courtesy Dearborn Press

10. Carry a small first aid kit. Having one available always seems to prevent serious accidents.

Once you've enjoyed several day adventures you might be willing to try a weekend camping trek!

14
Cycle Camping

By the time you've reached this section you should have retained some basic information about bicycles, clothing and organizational approach. If you've just opened this book and hit this section on cycle camping because you're going on a trip tomorrow, you deserve whatever pits into which you most surely will fall!

Preparation for cycle camping has to be as thorough as possible, but it offers by far the most wonderful, stimulating, loving passage for a very tiny glimpse of God's gift to nature.

For the routined regulated businessman, factory worker, secretary or housewife, it's one opportunity to sever any ties with the programmed life—at least for two weeks.

There's no need for any fixed schedule. If you hit a spot where you'll be happy spending the whole two weeks, great! You're not forced to move on because you've scheduled a hostel or hotel and you might lose ten bucks.

The real pleasure of this type of camping is listening to air bubbles break on rocks as they hurry down a small moss covered ledge or maybe tying your recently discovered cricket on a hook and line and watching an 18″ German Brown Trout affectionately eye this tidbit. And how long has it been since you listened to the song of wind blown leaves or wary leopard frogs, or smelled real cedar?

If you want to seek this solitude, it's going to take some planning. Again, for the beginner, I think 2 or 3 weekend trips with the American Youth Hostels will prepare you to deal with most problems. A bike "Atlas" published by the AYH contains over 100 long distance and weekend bi-

cycle tours with interesting descriptions of what can be seen along the routes. Fifty states, territories, Puerto Rico and Mexico are included in the Atlas. Write to the AYH headquarters and include $1.95 plus 30¢ postage.

I've led enough AYH trips to know that no trip is without some minor problem, but I've never had a trip that was an out and out disaster—even when it rained 3 out of 3 days, and we had 3 days of sauerkraut for dessert.

Rain? Whether you're touring or racing it's dangerous if you're moving fast. Turning too sharply, hitting a slippery pile of wet leaves, getting tossed by a water covered sewer grating, are all sure spills. Tires are narrow and don't provide much road grip. Rain is especially troublesome to people who wear glasses. They glob up from both rain and breath vaporizing . . . and if you don't have fenders, add road goop to the whole ugly mess.

If you're not in an area where you *can* obtain basic camping experience, read on. I've already discussed the best bicycle for camping. If you've skipped that section, check it out.

Planning: Never travel alone. Groups of 6 or 8 seem to work out best. It's easier to handle food preparation and break up job assignments. Children should be worked into the whole camping routine, too.

For family camping, be sure the children are responsible cyclists. If you have to "tote" a child there are several rear fender mounted child carriers that are adequate. Constantly check to be sure the frame clip stays secured and the child's feet are positioned to prevent contact with the rear wheel. Front child carriers are taboo as steering the bicycle is too critical.

Child Carriers

About "singles": I'm very much in favor of young unmarrieds roughing it together. Nothing brings out character faster than watching a prospective mate operate under reasonably primitive conditions. How many of us in the courting process have run into the situation where time spent with the opposite sex is always under ideal conditions; *i.e.*, showered, shaved, perfumed and pampered. When the honeymoon is over and they finally make it to the kitchen, he discovers she can't wash dishes and she discovers he can't cook.

I'll guarantee that by cycling together most of those horrible secrets will be both illuminated and resolved. If they can stand each other after a week of camping together, any prospective marriage should have a foundation of real character evaluation. Particularly after she's burned the night meal and they all sit munching crackers to fill the void.

Planning the route: Get the group together and decide where the tour will go. You might want to cycle right from your town. If you're from the

Camping Solitude—Courtesy Pat Mitchell

big city, you might want to pack your bicycles by plane or train. For either, remove both wheels, strap them to either side of the diamond frame and fold up in a canvas. Use a toe strap to close up the canvas. Occasionally the airlines will permit an assembled bicycle to be loaded, but 6 or 8 would never be accepted. Trains are a little

Bicycle Tote Bag

more lenient. Packaging also protects the derailleur and other parts. Whichever method you choose to initiate your trip, there's little problem.

Train Travel with Bicycles—Courtesy Al Hatos

When you've decided where you're going, contact the American Youth Hostels to see if they have any suggested routings or hostels in that area. If not, visit the local automobile association. They have available all sorts of road information, *i.e.*, the amount of car travel on roads, whether they're well paved or rotten gravel, whether there are camping sites with pure water or whether the mosquitoes annually devour unwary invaders. They can also provide specialized information about particular points of interest in this prospective travel zone.

If you're really adventurous with pints of pioneer blood in your arteries, you might want to write to that area's State Conservation Department. This agency and the U.S. Department of Interior publish county maps in detail that show abandoned trails, roads, mines, streams, special rock formations, etc. Generally this information is provided at nominal cost, about $1.00.

Personally, I feel beginners should keep some daily contact with civilization. This eliminates one of the biggest headaches for beginners, finding they've forgotten to pack a very essential item and are a six hour ride away from a place to purchase it. It also eliminates one of the biggest handicaps, packing huge amounts of food.

Once the group has selected the area they want to tour, check off available campsites, emergency stops or hostels, ranger stations or police headquarters and outline the best roads.

Contact the Conservation Department to see whether a dry season has ruled out camping, or a wet season has the local dam threatening to burst. If you intend to camp and tour in one particular section for a full week and use a base camp to tour from, the Conservation Department may even drop in to see if you need any assistance.

Remember to locate within rideable distance of a small town for your first stop. Forty to fifty miles *round-trip* should be the maximum for your first camp site. Packing groceries for three or four days for a group of six means two heavily loaded bicycles, and at the start of your tour you should plan to carry two day's supplies with you. This way camping procedure can be worked out without having two of the group miss out on the initial set-up routine needed to establish a well organized camp site.

Mileage: A well equipped camper should not exceed fifty to sixty miles a day, with one or two days of only thirty to forty miles. These miles can be travelled at approximately 15 m.p.h., with the 5 minute walk and the whole day's routing taking no more than 4 or 5 hours.

The group should get together at least two or three times prior to the trip to discover if anyone will run into problems in maintaining a schedule. Alterations to the program can always be made to accommodate those who are not such accomplished cyclists. Perhaps all that's needed is a reshifting of equipment to another rider who has muscles that just ooze energy. Make sure you have practiced two very important points:

1. Packing the bicycle efficiently, so it's balanced evenly with the frequently used items easily accessible.
2. Riding, stopping and starting *with a fully loaded bicycle.*

Travel Log: Before you leave the protection of civilization, a travel log should be set. Make sure that friends or relatives have a copy of your itinerary so that in an emergency, the State Police or Conservation Department will be able to locate your group.

Even though you might change some camping spot or decide to remain a few extra days in a particularly lovely area, the itinerary will give the searcher a good guide to use in quickly locating your campsite.

Equipment: After the bicycle, your first consideration should be the tent, and then the selection and *care* of other proper camping equipment related to cycle camping.

Tent: As with just about everything we know, there is no ultimate when it comes to tents. They continue to be redesigned for lightness, efficiency, warmth, and easy assembly, with

the latest of space age fabrics. Write the camping equipment specialists for their brochures on what's available. However, there are a few basic guidelines that have to be observed.

1. One or 2 man tents give the best performance and can keep the campsite reasonably orderly and neat. The tent should be lightweight, extremely waterproof and pack compactly. Figure on six to eight pounds for the two man tent and five to six pounds for the one man tent. In an emergency, the two man tent can sleep three reasonably comfortably, and the one man can sleep two. Wedge, Pyramid and Explorer type tents pitch easily and need a gale force wind to be blown down.
2. The tent should have a sewn-in floor to prevent drafts and surface moisture. The floor guards against snakes and other creepy crawlers.
3. It should have zip up mosquito netting in the doorway for air circulation on hot nights. The doorway should also have door flaps so it can be closed tight during inclement or cold weather. Make sure it has enough height so that during those inclement periods there is sufficient room for meal preparation and use of a portable stove.

   A note of caution: If you're forced to cook inside the tent during bad weather, be sure you have the tent door open to replace the oxygen that will be consumed by the stove.

Air mattress: What to sleep on? Well, only bears, deer and long-winded-non-campers indicate they prefer to sleep on the ground. No matter what the bedding, an air mattress can make the difference between eight nightly hours of comfort or two weeks of bleary-eyed misery.

Again, size, type and quality is a matter of preference, but I can guarantee that the discount store's 99¢ plastic special will puncture with the first sharp look. Nylon or rubber impregnated hold up well, and the nylon is lighter.

If there are six air mattresses to be blown up each evening, it's wise to carry one of those small accordian type mattress inflators. They weigh ap-

Air Mattress Inflator

Tents

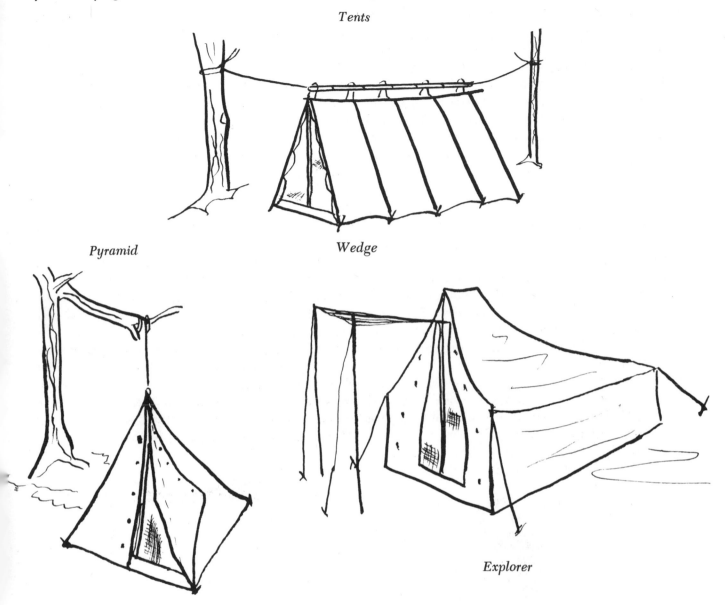

Pyramid

Wedge

Explorer

proximately seven ounces and can be tucked anywhere in the saddlebag.

Bedding: On top of that precious comfort-laden air bubble can be a variety of blankets, bags, liners, robes, rolls, etc. It's easy to use and adjust to different bedding as long as there's an air mattress accompanying it.

For those who are really going to do a good bit of camping, the 2 to 3 pound down bag is an investment that will give a lifetime of service and even be handed-down to the next generation of campers. This bag rolls-up tightly, packs neatly and provides a maximum of warmth without

weight. About the only difficulty encountered with a bag comes when the sleeper wants to turn over or change position; it's a little restrictive.

I had an interesting experience on my first three day camping trip at the age of 18. I had joined the American Youth Hostels, purchased my lovely new down bag and was ready for my first canoeing trip. Since I didn't want one speck of that dirty old ground to soil my nifty new bag, I bought umpteen yards of red plastic from an Army Surplus Store, and sewed a protective case for the bag. When it came time to bed down for the night I crawled fully clothed into my waterproof cocoon. Slowly I began to get more and more uncomfortable. . . . cold. By morning I was convinced that any duck who relied on feathers for warmth must know a few secrets I didn't.

When I finally crawled out fully clothed, I observed my companions in various stages of underwear climbing out of their own bags and seemingly in various stages of radiating warmth. So I did the obvious, I asked why the heck I was cold and they were warm.

Much to my surprise I was informed that by inadvertently waterproofing my bag, I had stopped it from breathing and then moisture from my body condensed, giving the effect of lying in slime. The other error was going to bed fully clothed. This made it impossible for the body to make its nice insulated layer of warmth. The final mistake was in not making a sheet sleeping sack. The sack saves the interior of the bag from soiling during those times when it's impossible to wash before that deep forty winks.

At the end of those three days I had to have the bag cleaned (which I did with soap and water). Nearly 20 years later I am still using the same bag and haven't had it as dirty as during those initial three days without the muslin sack. *Stoves:* For the individual, the Primus type that burns alcohol or kerosene is sufficient. It weighs only 2 1/2 pounds, holds two pints of fuel which normally burns 2 1/2 hours. It can boil a quart of water in 3 minutes. Any cyclist can easily carry enough fuel to get by for days.

For a group of six, one of the two burner aluminum Coleman type stoves is great. It's reasonably light, folds extremely compactly, and can operate on approximately 1/2 pint of fuel per burner per hour. Again, there will always be style and material changes that will improve these stoves, so be sure to look at all models available. Whatever you choose, practice with it *before* the trip.

A big illusion to dispense with right now is the romantic open campfire cooking nonsense. It's a hot, sticky, pan-blackening, spark-spitting nightmare that even experienced campers find disheartening.

It takes a good bit of know-how to determine how high the pots should be, how long the food should be cooking, and when the coals are just right so you can depend on them. However, it is one always available method of cooking and I'll discuss open fire cooking further along.

Hatchet

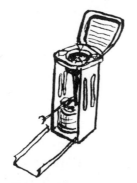

Primus Type Stove

Coleman Type Stove

Hatchet: Small sized ax. This item should be of good quality. Probably weighing around a pound and a half, it should have a good hardwood handle and fine steel head. There are dozens of uses for the ax beside chopping firewood. It can remove obstinate branches from the campsite, cut tent poles, pound like a hammer, fashion a table, clean game, dig a latrine, shave a branch for kindling, etc.

Trench Shovel: Folding, Army type. Necessary for trenching around the tents and easy latrine digging.

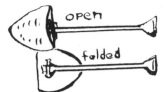

Trench Shovel

Camper Knife-Fork-Spoon Set

Camper Knife-Fork-Spoon Set: Suit your own taste on this item.

Jackknife: This should be of high carbon steel. It has lots of do-dads like a hole puncher, screw driver, can opener, cap lifter, file, in addition to a blade that can skin a deer or fillet a fish.

Mess Kit

Mess Kit: Should be of the nesting type that has two or three pans, cups, (some even include a little tea kettle) inside each other. Generally of aluminum, or other lightweight approved cooking material, some with "Teflon."

Wooden Spoon and Spatula: Ordinary household items, absolutely necessary for easy cooking.

Aluminum Foil Roll: For "over the coals" roasting.

Reflector Oven: Aluminum, for baking biscuits or pan bread.

Reflector Oven

Canteen

Canteen: Lots of styles available. *Don't forget the water-purifying pills, called halazone tablets:* Very necessary, very inexpensive.

Water Bucket

Folding Water Bucket: Canvas type, or plastic fold-up, for camp use.

Pots and Pans: Naturally you'll be able to use the mess kit for some cooking, but for a group of six, an additional twelve inch skillet and lid, four and six quart stew type pans and lids, and possibly a large coffee pot can be included. Bread can be baked in the skillet, and one meal dishes can be handled in the stew pots.

Cotton Gloves: Gardener's Type for the cook.

Waterproof Match Box and Matches: Any household container that's water tight will work if you don't want to buy a special case. Be sure to use the old wooden kitchen matches. They burn longer with a hotter flame.

Battery-Powered Light and Candles: Your battery powered light can be your clamp-on bicycle light, but don't forget the candles. If the light fails, candles won't . . . plus an added feature. . . . candles can be used to ignite damp wood.

Scouring Pad: Reusable metal or plastic type.

Dishtowel: "Handiwipes" are the best. They can

be used over and over, wash and dry quickly and don't sour as easily.

Detergent: Small bottle (plastic) goes a long way. Can be used to suds out clothing as well as doing dishes.

One Bar of Soap: Good for coating pan bottoms against soot, as well as generalized washing.

Nylon Rope: Fifty feet of nylon rope can be a lifesaver for trussing, broken straps, belts, emergency securing of any number of things.

First Aid Kit: Make your own. Don't buy one as they present a lovely packaged appearance with little value inside. What's really needed?

— Bandaids
— Gauze Pads
— Tape (Several rolls, good for 100 other jobs in the camp)
— Medicated ointment
— Calamine lotion
— Tincture of Merthiolate
— Small Scissors
— Tweezers
— Safety Pins
— Aspirin

Any big injury has to be treated professionally, so there's no need to carry anymore equipment *except:*

1. A small first aid book (the kind that explains how to handle severe injury until professional help can be reached.) Your local Red Cross Office has complimentary copies.
2. Personal specialized items like allergy medication. Some people are sensitive to bee stings. They need a special reaction treatment kit that can mean the difference between *life and death.*
3. Snake Bite Kit—It's seldom used, but provides a feeling of confidence.

Sewing Kit: Any watertight box with needles, thread and good quality fishing line for big jobs.

Insect Repellant: Bomb type for the tents shortly before retiring, rub-on or spray for the body. I like the Army rub-on liquid that comes from the Army-Navy Surplus Stores.

Box of Tissue: For Personal hygiene.

Note: The approximate weight of this equipment without the stove, is 28 pounds.

Cycle Equipment and Tools:

The independent cycle-camper should be prepared for some minor breakdowns. The following is a list supplied by the *Cyclo-Pedia Company:*

1. Tire Patch Kit
2. Tire Irons (for clincher tires)
3. 6″ Crescent Wrench
4. Offset Pliers (small)
5. Brass Screw Driver with assorted heads.
6. Spare tube (for clincher tires)
7. Spare tire (for clincher or tubular)
8. Tube bicycle grease
9. Six spokes and nipples (can be carried inside handlebar)
10. Two Brake Blocks
11. One Gear Cable—Rear (can be cut short for front)
12. One Brake Cable—Rear (can be cut short for front)
13. One plastic bike protector (A rain poncho can double for this)
14. Two 40″ webbed straps or Sandow stretch straps
15. Map measurer and compass
16. Bicycle Cable Lock
17. Small can Oil
18. Pump

Tools should be rolled in a "Handiwipe" which can double for a polishing cloth for the bicycle. Weight of tools is approximately 3 pounds.

Clothing and personal equipment—Men's List:

1. 2 pr. of socks
2. 2 pr. of Underwear (two shorts, two shirts)
3. 1 pr. of dress slacks
4. 1 modern fabric sports shirt
5. 1 light wool shirt or loose knit sweater
6. 1 pr. jeans or knock-around type pants, denim or duck type material
7. 1 pr. of dress loafers or good sneakers
8. Sunglasses
9. Extra pair of prescription glasses
10. Cap with visor
11. Suspenders (Most men prefer a belt, but suspenders prevent the waist from being rubbed raw while cycling or doing the regular camp chores.)
12. Cycling Tights (They come equipped with the buttons necessary to accommodate sus-

Weekend Campers—Courtesy Bill Olsen

penders.) They can also double as a bathing suit.

13. Hip length waterproof windbreaker type jacket
14. Poncho type rain cape (doubles for bike protector)
15. Toothbrush and paste
16. Soap and soap container
17. Wash cloth
18. Terry cloth hand towel
19. Razor and blades
20. Comb
21. Polished stainless steel mirror
22. Watch
23. Deodorant
24. Camera and film (35 m.m. seems to be the best to pack)

Approximate weight 5 pounds.

Women's List:

Before we get into the items, forget the girdle and up-lift bra. Comfort and efficiency are the two main concerns when it comes to packing clothes for two weeks.

1. 2 comfortable bras
2. 2 pr. comfortable panties
3. 1 pr. cotton underwear (like thermal shirt and long johns) if you seem to mind cool evenings)
4. 1 short sleeved, long tailed synthetic materialed shirt.

5. 1 long sleeved, long tailed light wool shirt or sweater.
6. 1 pr. jeans or knockaround pants (make sure the waist is loose so you can stuff in the added shirt.) Denim or duck type material.
7. Suspenders (belts rub the waist raw)
8. Cycling Tights (they come equipped with the buttons necessary to accommodate suspenders)
9. Bathing suit
10. 1 pr. socks
11. 2 pr. footies
12. 1 jersey dress (or light non-wrinkling material)
13. 1 pr. sandals or dress shoes
14. Scarf. It can also double as a sling in an emergency.
15. Sunglasses
16. Extra pair of prescription glasses
17. Hip length waterproof windbreaker type jacket
18. Poncho type rain cape (doubles for bike protector)
19. Toothbrush and paste
20. Deodorant
21. Make-up (limit this to basics)
22. Soap and soap container
23. Terry cloth hand towel
24. Wash cloth
25. Razor and blades
26. Comb
27. Polished Stainless Steel Mirror
28. Watch
29. Camera and film (35 m.m. seems to be the best to pack)

Approximate weight 5 pounds.

A few additional thoughts that apply to both sexes. If you are under some constant medication, make sure you have a complete supply, or a prescription that can be refilled.

A gentle reminder about clothing, again for either sex: be sure the clothing is not skin tight. Pants, particularly, can destroy circulation if the waist, crotch or legs are skin tight. Try to do without cuffs on the pants, because they're dirt and mud catchers, they eventually empty themselves in your tent. Cuffs also tend to get caught in the chainwheel unless they're restricted with a pants clip around the bottom.

Camping procedure:

If someone in your group intends to fish while on the cycle-camping trip, make sure he or she has the appropriate license necessary. Forest rangers stick very strongly to the rule that ignorance is no excuse. Common sense rules make up a great part of the regulations that affect campers.

As an example, when you pitch your camp near a lake or stream, be wary about camping right on the edge. Not only does it entice amphibious visitors, but a flash flood or rain storm can result in your loss of equipment or life.

Make sure the area you have chosen has adequate protection from gale winds and excellent drainage. Dig accessory ditches around the tents to be sure, and before raising those tents, check the area for protruding sticks or stones that could puncture the tent bottom. Also be alert for ant hills or wasp dens.

You should be familiar enough with your tent that you can pitch it easily, and fold it efficiently in the correct manner for its repacking. If you have more than one tent, try and keep one specifically for cooking and storing.

In *any* tent, remember to remove shoes before entering, or crawl in carefully on your hands and knees. This is one sure way of keeping the tent dirt free and bug free.

Routine for the group of six should begin by splitting up the assignments *before* leaving for the trip. However, everyone should be familiar with *all* the chores.

An easy break-up of job assignments can be as follows:
1. *One cook*
2. *Two* tent erectors
3. *One* blowing up air mattresses
4. *One* gathering wood for fire and water for cook.
5. *One* digging latrine and garbage pit.

Cook: This the one job that is managed best by a specific person, all the time. Other jobs can be switched between the other members of the group, with *everyone* having a turn at doing dishes.

The cook should have 2 day's meals planned and packaged for the initial camp set-up. This is a reasonable guarantee that no one will go hungry for two days, anyway. The

1. TINDER

2. SMALL TWIGS

3. LOGS - 4"-5" THICK

WIND DIRECTION →
LIGHT HERE —————

Building a fire

cook should also have tentative meals planned for the other twelve days, knowing exactly how much will be required to feed a group of six. What the cook decides upon should be tempered by what the whole group likes to eat. Find out *before* making menus! There are limitations on what can be prepared, but I've included one day's sample menu (See Page 94).

The first part of the cook's routine should be clearing the cooking site to suit the needs. He can build a temporary work area to facilitate preparation and serving. Even the poncho can help serve as a food preparation center. I'd make sure it's the cook's poncho though, so any leftover mustard greens around the collar can't be blamed on others. This poncho can also double as a cooking lean-to in inclement weather.

If the cook plans to use a campfire to cook over, he should gather rocks to form a key-hole type of campfire. In this arrangement, the rocks are laid in the form of a key with the fire built in the big end and then the coals moved down to the long narrow end where the cooking will be done.

This allows for both a campfire (with the large end kept going) and a cooking spot.
A word of caution: Select rocks that are from high ground, away from moisture. Rocks absorb moisture and can explode when heated.

Another outdoor cooking method is to dig a trench, line the trench with rocks, build a fire and when the wood has become coals place those items for roasting (wrapped in aluminum foil) over the coals. When there aren't rocks available, the pit and plain coals is sufficient although the heat is not as intense. In all my years of camping I've used only these methods when forced to cook without a camp stove.

To ignite a fire in wet weather, use the shaved stick method of splintering a dead bough, or any chunks of wood with pitch.

Shaved Stick

It might be wise to acquaint yourself with the types of wood that burn best:
Apple, Ash, Birch, Dogwood, Holly, Locust, Maple, Oak

If it is raining, the bicycle raincoat-poncho can be rigged to shelter the fire. Here is where the candle (or a small amount of bicycle oil) can be helpful.

To build the fire that makes enough coals for cooking, the Pyramid type seems to be the best. Tinder of twigs, leaves, etc., is placed in a bunch and then the wood to be burned is raised in a tee-pee or pyramid fashion.

Key Hole Campfire

If there's a good wind blowing, light the tinder upwind so that the flame will blow right into the tinder.

The hardest part of cooking is to wait until there are coals. Beginners usually burn everything with their impatience to *wait* until this happens. It takes experience, but it takes just as much patience!

Menus:

To begin with, if you can get away with instant coffee with your group, make up a batch of dried brew at home:

> One Part Coffee
> One Part Sugar
> One Part Powdered Milk

Mix it all up, and to serve, just a tablespoon per 8 oz. cup.

When heating canned goods, place cans in water, bringing the water to a boil, remove the cans, open and serve. Save any canned broth and use it for soups or stews if that's the day's menu.

Consider all of the dehydrated products: Eggs, onions, potatoes, milk, fruit. Most of these can be obtained from your supermarket; however, there are food specialists that service campers.

Preparations like "Bisquick" can round out meals. It can make biscuits, camp bread, desserts, gravy, pancakes, and coatings for frying.

Be familiar with the length of time necessary to cook certain cuts of meat. For instance, if a stew is planned the meat has to be cooked three-quarters through before the potatoes, carrots and onions are added.

Little packages of gravy mix, marinades and sauces (dry style) add a great deal to any cooked dish.

A roast can be rolled several times in aluminum foil and placed directly on the coals. Potatoes and corn can be treated in the same manner. About the same amount of time is required for this roasting as for oven roasting. Remember to turn about every 15 minutes.

For open campfire cooking, coat the outside pot or pan bottoms with bar soap or clay. This helps eliminate some of the black soot residue.

While the meal is being served, have water in all the cook pots to loosen stuck-on residue. At the same time, begin to boil water for washing dishes. If you're by a stream or river, pots can be rubbed out with sand and grass before the soap water cleaning.

Make it a camp rule that each person must clean his or her plate with a scrap of bread or biscuit before it's given to the dishwasher.

If possible, let dishes dry by themselves. It's the most sanitary way.

After the dishwashing is completed, pour the dirty water into the garbage trench. Nothing draws bugs quicker than greasy food remnants, so cover it with a layer of dirt.

The cook should be responsible for food storage as well. This can be handled in the equipment tent or by hanging it in a sack from a tree.

Sample Menu: Breakfast

Fresh orange, dehydrated eggs, sausage, pan bread or toast, coffee, or tea.

A. After cycling an hour or two, have a space food stick.

Lunch

Local fruit in season, campers sandwich, coffee, tea or milk.

A. Again, after more cycling, another space food stick.

Supper

Camp stew, pasta or rice, pan bread, canned or fresh fruit, coffee or tea.

A. Pre-bedtime, a cool baked potato well saturated with butter, sprinkled with salt, pepper and parmesan cheese, or fruit.

Breakfast Suggestions:

Coffee—If you prefer real brew:

> 8 tablespoons coffee (For 6 servings)
> 7 8 oz. cups of water

Start with cold water and coffee, bring to boil, reduce heat and simmer one minute. Usually the coffee grounds settle to the bottom, but if you're real finicky, use a tea strainer.

Bacon—Figuring two slices per person that's 12, so you may have to do two batches, saving the grease in a container for other uses. Fry over moderate heat, pouring off grease as it collects, once or twice during the frying. Remove bacon to foil wrap to keep warm.

Eggs—I believe in using the concentrated eggs, figuring 1/2 pound equalling about 2 dozen eggs. *Buy the best quality;* it really makes a difference. For six people, use the full half pound.

Approx. 6 Tablespoons dry milk
1 Teaspoon salt
1/2 Teaspoon pepper
3 1/2 Cups water

Mix all together. Beat until smooth. Pour the mixture into the skillet with about 2 Tablespoons hot bacon grease.

A. You can cook slowly and fold over like an omelette—or
B. Stir for scrambles.

Check the manufacturer's directions for different combinations. Each brand has its own directions.

Pan Bread—(Biscuits)

4 Cups Bisquick
1 Cup Cold Water

Mix lightly, drop by Tablespoonsful into skillet, cover and cook over moderate heat. Don't lift lid for about six minutes, then check to see if they're done. They spread together, so can be flipped to brown the tops if that's desired.

If you like the bacon flavor, add two Tablespoons of melted bacon grease while mixing the batter.

Lunchtime Suggestions:

You'll probably be cycling during the lunchtime hour, so the best things to plan on are those that can be prepared ahead and eaten cold. A favorite of everybody who has ever camped is the regular Camper's Sandwich Spread. Make up a batch before leaving on the trip. It keeps two to three weeks.

2 Cups Raisins
2 Cups Peanut Butter
1/2 Cup Butter
Dash of Salt

Grind raisins, mix with peanut butter and softened butter. Pack in airtight plastic container.

Canned Corned Beef Sandwiches (Or Spam, or Pork, Chicken, etc.)

Open can, slice on bread buttered with mustard or butter and serve.

Fruit

Dried or Fresh
Canned fruit provides additional juice for that liquid boost.

Supper Suggestions:

Stew

For a group of six:
Brown 3 Pounds of fresh stewing beef (or whatever quality you want)
Add 2 cups of boiling water. Cook covered to simmer about an hour.
Add 1/2 cup dehydrated onions (soaked for about 1/2 hour in water)
2 Cups dehydrated potatoes (soaked for about 1/2 hour in water)
Another cup of water if needed
1 package of instant gravy, onion or whatever mix you like, and cook for another 1/2 hour.
Add 1 Can of cut green beans just before serving (with water).
Mix well to make sure they're heated through.
Serve with biscuits, instant rice or noodles.

Variations on a theme—Use canned meat. When using canned meat, do the dehydrated vegetables first, add the gravy mix, canned meat and green beans just before serving, making sure everything is heated through.

Spaghetti (For six)

Soften dehydrated onion (1/2 cup)
Saute until golden brown in 3 tablespoons fat
Add 3 lbs. hamburger (or whatever grade of beef you like)
Brown well with onion
Skim off grease
Add 1 can tomato paste and water for sauce texture (about 1 1/2 cups)
Add 1 tablespoon parsley flakes, salt and pepper to taste (I like the seasoned salt and pepper) and 1 Tsp. MSG.
Simmer about 1/2 hour.
Add cooked, drained spaghetti, mix well and serve.

Variation:

—Use noodles or rice instead of spaghetti.

—Add two cans of kidney beans (#303 size) and 2 Tablespoons of Chili Powder for Chili instead of Spaghetti

—Skip tomato paste, add two packages Stroganoff Sauce over browned hamburger. Add three cups of water with one cup of powdered milk dissolved in it. Bring back to boil, stirring until thick, serve over mashed potatoes, rice or noodles.

Steaks, pork chops, lamb chops (For six)
Six portions, cooked to taste. (Pork should always be well done.)
Serve with canned tomatos, instant mashed potatoes, gravy mix, pan bread, canned vegetables.

Fish

Any fish planned for cooking will naturally be caught wherever your camp site is located. It's impossible to buy fish and then cart them 5 hours on a bicycle in 85° heat. . . . unless they're canned. The bicycle will stink and the botulism will kill.

Fresh Fish!—Courtesy John Mitchell

The sooner a fish is cooked the tastier it is, and some fish like catfish and bass should be gutted and skinned immediately after being caught for best flavor. Certainly you can't always get trout or perch, but I'd forget carp. I've had

them prepared by "experts" and still find it hard to get the second mouthful past the lips. But then each person's appreciation of game fish is different from the next.

There are three methods to handle fish while camping. My favorite is pan fry in butter.
Pan fried fish
    3 pounds of filleted fish (serve 6)
    Parsley (about 2 tablespoons)
    2 teaspoons of salt
    1/4 teaspoon pepper
Melt 1/4 pound butter, dip fish fillets in milk then in cracker crumbs or flour that has the salt and pepper mixed in, fry at moderate heat 3 to 5 minutes or until light brown. Turn fish carefully, brown second side about 3 minutes. Dot with parsley, Serve immediately.
Baking fish
Very simple. Place 3 pounds of fish in shallow baking pan (or lay on aluminum foil for cooking over coals). Dot with butter, salt, pepper. Cover, or wrap closed with aluminum foil. Use moderate hot heat on stove, place directly on coals for campfire cooking about 20 minutes. For a terrific variation, add 1/2 cup of dry sauterne!
Broiled Fish
    3 pounds of filleted fish. Rub with a good grade of olive oil, place on broiling rack over hot coals. Fillets under an inch thick cook in about 10 minutes, need turning only once. Thicker sections take about 15 minutes, but should only be turned once. Keep fish about 2 inches above the coals, basting again with olive oil after turning. Season with salt and pepper.

If you have nice large fish, pan dress the fish and then fill and baste with a sauce of 1 mashed garlic clove, 1/2 cup olive oil, 1 cup tomato sauce, 1 tablespoon parsley, 1/2 teaspoon salt, 1/8 teaspoon pepper.

For a good all-round fish meal that serves 6, try a chowder (or stew). It can have many variations and like a stew can use many different vegetables.
Celery chowder
Use 1 1/2 to 2 pounds of any variety white meated filleted fish. Place in deep kettle, cover with 1 1/2 cups of cold water.

Simmer over medium heat 10 minutes or until

fish is easily flaked with a fork. Remove, flake and place flaked fish in another large pot. Pour off fish water, save for later.

Place 4 tablespoons of butter in kettle, add 1 large chopped onion and saute until golden brown. Add 2 large diced potatos, 3 ribs of celery and 1 1/4 cups of water. Add one teaspoon of your favorite seasoning sauce, Worcestershire, A-1, etc., cover and cook 15 minutes or until vegetables are tender.

Blend 4 tablespoons of flour with 2 cups of milk; when smooth, add 2 more cups of milk, then add to the vegetables. Add fish, stock and heat to boiling but do not boil. Season with salt and pepper, serve immediately.

Note: Most cookbooks have a section devoted to outdoor cooking and many American Youth Hostel Councils publish their own. Remember that most indoor ideas can be used outdoors as long as no specialized cooking equipment is needed.

> *A rule of thumb:* Always calculate 1/2 pound of meat for each person. Some eat more, others less, so it balances out.

> *Additional mealtime suggestions:*—Make sure there's an ample supply of fruit, dried or canned, fresh if possible. Getting constipated is no pleasure at any time, let alone cycling.

> Take a supply of vitamin pills. Good for mental reassurance if nothing else.

B. *Tent erectors*—These two should be responsible for choosing and clearing the site for the tents. They should be familiar with the assembly and dismantling, and repacking of the tents. Tent erectors should also read a few tent manuals on how to patch holes in emergency situations.

C. *Air mattress inflator*—This individual (who wisely packed an accordian type inflator) should be the first to complete the assignment and ready to help pitch in with the others. He might be assigned the job of digging the tent drainage system.

D. *Wood gatherer and water carrier*—Should be aware of the best kinds of wood for campfires. He should be familiar with these on sight, knowing which types make the best tinder, which start best in wet weather and

Getting Ready for Comfort—Courtesy Jessie Miley

how to chop wood. And, there is no such thing as too much wood. He should be a "helper" if the group uses a Coleman stove.

The folding canvas water bucket should be filled immediately for the cook's use, and kept full for camp convenience.

E. *Latrine and garbage pit digger*—This is where the small trench shovel is invaluable. You can manage with an ax and a lot of effort, but the shovel makes it so easy.

To begin with, the latrine should be at least 200 feet from the campsite. Pick a couple of trees that are reasonably close together, tie two branches (sturdy ones that can be

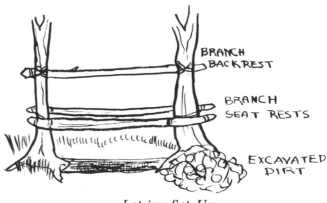

Latrine Set-Up

sat on) so they join the two trees and form sort of a bench type arrangement. This is another place where that nylon line comes in handy.

Dig a fairly deep hole, piling all the loose ground in a neat pile so it can be used to cover the refuse after each use.

It's bad enough to come across bear droppings, let alone a filthy campsite visited by some ignorant, lazy, campers. Make sure your latrine is completely covered before moving on to the next site.

The garbage pit should be dug at least 100 feet from the tent area, and all canned goods, glass or unburnable refuse should be deposited here. Water from the dishpan should be deposited here as well, and it's a good idea to burn trash in the pit occasionally to discourage the small scavenger animals from digging things out for food.

The garbage pit should be covered over with the last of the dirt before moving on to the next site.

In discussing all of the above jobs, it should be understood that gender is not involved with job description. It very well may be that the man will be the best cook and the woman the best tent erector or latrine digger, and most certainly everyone should take a turn at one or the other jobs just to become familiar with all the little sidelines of each routine.

Dishwashing: This is one job that should be shifted between all members, unless there is someone who specifically likes to wash dishes and does them well. A few simple but very important rules:

1. Every member turns over a plate that has been wiped free of all food.
2. The water with which to wash the dishes should be warming while the meal is being eaten.
3. If there are any pots or pans that have goop stuck in them, they should be soaking while the meal is being eaten.
4. Scrape all this grease and goop into the garbage pit before the actual washing.
5. If possible, use sand and leaves to wipe the pans reasonably clean.
6. Begin by washing the least soiled items first in your water that has a good detergent. If you have another pan that can be used to dip rinse, keep the water close to boiling and dip and then set the dishes to dry by themselves on the makeshift table.

Garbage cover-up—Courtesy John Mitchell

Dish Washing Chores—Courtesy Pat Mitchell

7. If you have only one pan available, rinse the dishes clear of the soap residue in the stream or river and then boil some water in that one pan to pour over the rinsed dishes as a sterilizing agent.

8. Dishtowels are a no-no. They just can't be kept clean enough to prevent bacteria from developing. Leftover soap residue or bacteria gathering food residue can produce disastrous gastrointestinal inflammation.

Clothes Washing

In a two week period, there will have to be some clothes washing done. The majority of the problem will be with the underclothing, tee shirts, socks and shorts, etc., that get the perspiration odors as well as the coffee spills. These can be lightly suds out at night, hung on the branches, bushes or over the bicycle frames to dry. Heavier dirt or grease stains can be put up with for two weeks, or they can be saturated with detergent overnight and then rinsed out in the morning.

Clothes Washing Blues—Courtesy Jessie Miley

Packing the bicycle

The total weight of complete equipment for a *lone* cyclist is approximately 35 pounds. However, when travelling in a group, the weight would drop because some of the items would not have to be duplicated. For instance, the tent, stove, camp ax, compass, first aid kit, shovel, repair tools, spare tire and tube, large pots or pans, sewing kit, maps, nylon rope, dish towel, folding water bucket, scouring pad, cotton gloves, reflector oven, steel mirror are one-of-a-kind items.

Pannier Bags: These are the bags that fit over the rear carrier like saddle bags. They have to be waterproofed and designed so the rider's heel will not hit the bag while pedalling.

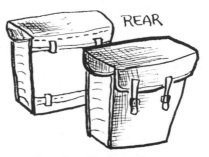

Pannier Cycling Bags

A large rear bag can be attached to the saddle and a front carrier bag is attached over the front carrier and attached to the handlebar.

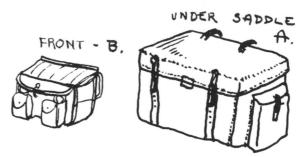

Bicycle Bags—A. Saddle Bag; B. Bar Bag

Nothing should be back-packed. It is extremely difficult and dangerous to keep that fine control of the bicycle with a shifting load on your back. The illustrated, packed bicycle gives an idea of how the loaded bicycle can be outfitted.

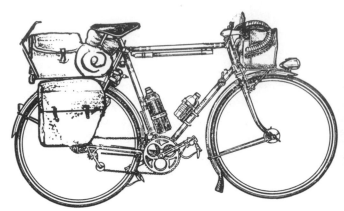

Loaded Bicycle

That last cup of coffee!—Courtesy Pat Mitchell

Clothes should be rolled as compactly as possible with socks, shorts, tee shirts, towels, soap, etc., placed inside pots and pans. Some items can even be rolled in the sleeping bag.

Practice packing the bags several times before the actual trip. Even placement of luggage ensures a well distributed load for easy cycling.

For example, if a Coleman type stove is carried, it would be best to strap it to the top of the rear luggage carrier instead of placing it in one of the saddle bags. This would prevent a lopsided load.

In closing the section on bicycle camping, remember these basic instructions should be tempered with wisdom and golden rule usage.

Use your library, conservation departments and police department for additional research. Get all you can, read all you can, and then have fun!

BICYCLE CAMPING, NANCY BARANET STYLE

I have to devote some thought to the kind of camping I personally find stimulating and relaxing. It's bicycling, motel camping and eating out. With the small children I really dig this, but I'm outvoted five to one. However, it certainly is worth mentioning.

15
Cycling in the School Physical Fitness Program

If you're really interested in having cycling included as a part of your grade school child's fitness program, be prepared to put out a very great effort for a very small return. There are few schools in the kindergarten through twelve grade system that have any cycling at all, and even fewer who include it on a regular basis.

Elementary School Instruction—Courtesy Nick Baranet

I can give a list of ten good reasons why they don't include cycling as a part of the athletic program, but I'd rather give ten good ones why they should:
1. It's healthy exercise for keeping physically fit.
2. It will improve motor control, conditioning and endurance.

3. It has goals attainable by ALL children, not just those physically gifted. Even the *least* physically endowed will achieve.
4. It is not a "contact" sport like football, hockey or wrestling that many times has it's participants plastered with nasty injuries.
5. It emphasizes group cooperation.
6. It teaches some mechanical theories and involves children with proper use of many basic tools.
7. It is an educational media for prospective automobile drivers.
8. It's an inexpensive method of transportation to and from school and just might reduce the juvenile "car need" syndrome.
9. It broadens the rider's self reliance and increases maturity by enabling the rider to explore without use of the family automobile.
10. It gives all parents an opportunity to devote some time and become involved in classroom procedure.

If you're a real masochist and want to initiate a program, begin by stimulating student interest and then organize the parents. You can have the best program in the world, but if you approach the school administration alone it's dead before you can say "hello." Approach with a group of one hundred interested parents and children, and watch the active interest ooze out of the school staff.

Start by getting the children involved. If you can't sell the kids, don't waste time with the adults. Nothing is worse than having forty pairs of eyes look at you with "here's another warped program the over-the-hill-group has dreamed up."

School "Parking" Lot—Courtesy Nick Baranet

Who wants to do something because "it's good for you?" Mothers the world over have wiped out any incentive with this phrase.

For the high school group, say it's "sexy". . . . not that "physical appeal can be encouraged and refined through correct exercise." You might even imply that cycling makes one more virile. That should sell it to 95% of the group; the other 5% are dead.

Grade schoolers are much easier to convince. Anything new, anyway they can let off steam plus the added touch of beginning a new "fad," will be appreciated.

Procedure:

Once you have some interested students, initiate the program with the school by asking for a meeting with the Principal, Athletic Director, PTA Officers, and a zillion parents.

Go with a completely prepared program covering items that could be fitted into one semester's planning. That gets you, doesn't it! But it's not as difficult as it sounds. Here's an example:

A. Ask that one or two periods a week be used as a part of the athletic fitness program for cycling.

B. Be prepared to assist the teacher at each session, with additional personnel if possible.

Once the program is moving along nicely, the Athletic Director can determine the personnel requirements.

C. On both the grade and high school levels, the children will be asked to ride their bicycles to school on the days that they are to have their cycling class. The bicycles can be placed in a special section of the school's bicycle rack so they're easily accessible.

Scheduling:

The first session should be orientation, without bicycles, explaining the program, types of activities (rides, movies, competition, safety and maintenance programs, etc.), clothing required, homework assignments contemplated. Ask the children to keep a separate notebook for their cycling classes, recording each session's activities. They can reserve a section for safety and clinic information, as well as keeping a log on the types of events ridden, number of miles covered and whether or not they enjoyed the activity. Any additional outside homework or cycling assignments should also be noted.

Two by two—Courtesy Nick Baranet

The second session should get right into the actual riding. A beginning program could have the group pair off by twos, ride a selected path around the school property and practice safety instructions, rider signals, etc. Plan to adjust any ill fitting bicycles and if possible, spend a few minutes with each rider and bicycle to note any particular maintenance or repair problem that might be discovered.

The third session might be a continuation of the second if it is a big group, or perhaps a movie might be scheduled.

The fourth session can be a safety clinic. Your local Police Department is very interested in reaching the pre-car youth. They have safety literature, films, and will work directly with the children in signal instruction and good bicycling habits. Groups of six or eight with an adult leader seem to work out best.

The fifth session can be a group interest bicycle program (see Programming). You can't hit the children with too much programming, but too much clinic and maintenance stuff will warp the program.

I'm in favor of having one class a month devoted to the clinic and safety items. The children themselves will be coming up with some whopping problems that will have to be handled in a clinic atmosphere.

When it rains on that day you've scheduled for programmed cycling, have a cycling movie available.

The Sixth Session—and on—Programming

1. Slow Races (Who can take the longest time to complete a course without touching or crossing the guidelines).
2. Obstacle Races (Around tin cans, who can do the best time).
3. Team Races (Two teams, 15 or 20 on a team engaged in a relay type of event. Winning team is the first to finish the relay, and any type of events can be developed).
4. Stunts (How many rings can be picked up with a stick while covering a specified course.)
5. Fast Races (Best time for a specified distance).
6. Coasting Races (Who can coast the furthest from a specific starting point).
7. Riding the strip race (Rider has to stay inside the 8" wide riding strip).
8. Rides to local points of interest or just plain sight-seeing rides.
9. Invent your own rides with ideas from the group.

Slow Race Start—Courtesy Paul Gach

Field Day—Courtesy Paul Gach

10. Cookouts, campouts, field-days, rodeos.

Remember, there isn't any one activity that will appeal to everyone. By using imagination and available resources, the program will have something for everyone, and if the group is stimulated with unlimited programs and leadership, success is guaranteed. Hopefully, the enthusiasm, health and fitness generated through the grade and high school programs will involve many parents. Those who do become involved certainly will benefit as much from the activities as the students.

If some type of competitive urge is aroused, it can be channelled into intra-mural activities at first and then inter-scholastic ones. A best-all-rounder program for each school can be developed by awarding points for different levels of achievement. Eventually there may be those who will go on into national competition and may even make an Olympic team.

Our main interest should be just for plain old bicycling and its own enjoyment. Don't set goals that are out of reach for the majority of the group, it has to be fun and rewarding at each level. Good luck!

Additional program listings can be had by writing:

> American Association of Health, Physical Education and Recreation
> 1201—16th Street
> Washington 36, D.C.

Awards and program helps for your school events can be obtained by writing on your organization's letterhead to:

Bicycle Institute of America
Mr. John Auerbach
122 E. 42nd Street
New York, N.Y., 10017

If you can interest anyone in popping funds to develop a velodrome, the Huffman Manufacturing Company, Dayton, Ohio, publishes a *Handbook on Bicycle Tracks and Cycle Racing,* that can most adequately cover the actual physical requirements.

College Racing—If you want to race in college you're just about on your own. College teams are usually made up of licensed Amateur Bicycle League of America cyclists who are going to school. They generally spend their own money for everything with little support from the college. Unfortunately money speaks very loudly and most athletic departments put their money where it's going to show a visible return.

Good salesmanship goes a long way though, and many of the colleges sponsoring teams do supply them with a room for equipment storage, uniforms (generally it's only a printed T-shirt) and occasionally an allowance for equipment maintenance. One man can't sell the program, it takes a combined effort of really enthusiastic young men, who can approach an athletic department with:

A. There are X-number of us cyclists who want to represent this college.

B. Although there is no possibility of a financial gain, we can guarantee good newspaper publicity, coverage on TV and writeups in the Trade Publications and College Papers.

C. There are X-number of races we will be attending this year, here is a list. Scoring points in these races will give us the opportunity of winning a National Team or Individual Championship for this college. As individuals we can also win recognition for the college through placing on an Olympic, Pan American or World Championship team.

D. We plan an active membership development program and will assist in educating campus members in the healthful, ecology dedicated sport of bicycling. We can help organize touring groups and assist them in developing proper cycling technique.

With these goals in mind, we would like:

*Henry Ford Community College Cyclist and 1970
Michigan State Road Racing Champion, Paul Gach—
Courtesy Howard Humphries*

A. A room for storing bicycles, tools, equipment
and a postal box for incoming mail.
B. College Uniforms
C. Financial support for:
   1. Cost of membership for club in Amateur
   Bicycle League of America. (Registered
   clubs get the benefit of all League mail-
   ings.)
   2. License Registration.
   3. Entry Fees for events.
   4. Transportation (or mileage allotment for
   a private car that can manage the team).
   5. Equipment—This is a variable. You might

just want to ask for an equipment allotment
to take care of maintenance and repairs. I
don't believe there is presently any college
team receiving complete equipment coverage.
   6. Athletic recognition in the form of varsity
   letter.
   7. Financial assistance for participation in specialized training camps.

These are the major give-and-take bargaining
points for a college team. You might only end up
with basic school recognition, which could be
just a letter from your athletic director stating
"Max Tax is a registered student at Bona Fida U.,
and can represent this University in all college
cycling competition." But if you do well under
these circumstances you can probably squeeze

College Cyclists scoring publicity at Kettering, Ohio—
Courtesy Howard Humphries

something out of the athletic director the following year.

Remember that to race you must hold a license,
and this has to come from the Amateur Bicycle
League of America. Furthering your college cause
takes involvement in recruiting membership, planning scheduled activities, holding sanctioned
events, and much conversation with college administration. That might call for several hours
weekly of time devoted to involvement that isn't
training or racing itself. Many young people who
are forced to work for their education are on a
tight time or money schedule and just can't afford
to donate their time to helping build the activity.
Don't bite off more than you can chew. Begin
easily and feel your way the first year. Be realistic
in how much of you can be given freely and then
build from there.

16

Amateur Bicycle Racing

Amateur bicycle racing in the United States is controlled through the Amateur Bicycle League of America (ABL of A). It was organized in 1920 and incorporated in 1921 after a long fight for freedom from the professionals who controlled cycling. One of the grand men who rode at that time and kept cycling going through the Depression and World War II is Otto "Spots" Eisele, who continues to ride and write for cycling.

The ABL of A licenses all amateur racing cyclists and sanctions all competitive events. It also annually promotes the State and National Championships, is responsible for the Pan American and Olympic Trials every four years, and develops a team program for the annual World Championships.

What is an amateur? "An amateur sportsman is one who engages in sport solely for the pleasure, and physical, mental or social benefits he derives therefrom."

Competitors fall into the following categories:
Veterans—40 years of age and over
Senior Men—18 years of age and over
Junior Men—15 years of age until 18th birthday
Intermediate Boys—12 years of age until 15th birthday
Midget Boys—8 years of age until 12th birthday
Senior Women—15 years of age and over
Intermediate Girls—12 years of age until 15th birthday
Midget Girls—8 years of age until 12th birthday
All of this information may seem rather dry, but it's the basis for every bit of racing or training that's done in the states today. Everybody who races has the ultimate goal of being National,

Olympic, Pan American or World Championship contestant, and how to get there is the purpose of this section.

Begin by obtaining your racing license. Your local library will always have the listing of the organization's current address. Write directly to the President who will refer the request to your State Representative. The State Representative will forward the application form and also give you a listing of the local clubs. There is a charge for the racing license and the application will advise you of the current charge. Enclose an extra $1.00 for the ABL of A Rules and Regulations.

Now you're registered, have the rules, but where to go? The definition of "amateur" dwells on pleasure and social benefits. Most champions want more. They want that thrill of competition and satisfaction of success. It's natural to want to succeed, but we aren't all of the same temperament.

Racing bicycles blends nicely with this because there are many different types of competition for the racer to examine.

Types of Racing—In the United States there are two basic categories of racing that require different training methods.

A. *Road Racing* (Held on open road, closed course or specialized circuit)

B. *Track Racing* (Held on enclosed velodrome)

A. *Road Racing:* A group of riders massed together at the start of the race on an open road or closed circuit course, for a predetermined distance, with the first man across the finish line declared the winner.

A.B.L. of A. Past President, Otto "Spots" Eisele

Then

Now

B. Track Racing: Racing either individually or *en masse* on an enclosed velodrome, with numerous variations in competitive events.

There are other offshoots of cycling, but they are seldom held in this country and generally not a part of the National Championships, although they can appear as Pan American, Olympic or World Championship events.

Road Time Trialing: An individual or group (usually limited from 2 to 4 riders) riding on a measured certified course, trying to do the fastest time possible for that distance. Generally, the riders (or teams) are separated by 30 seconds or longer so there is none of the advantage of pace from other riders.

Roller Racing: Riding the rollers with a clock attachment that gives visual evidence of the rider's progress. Usually done during the winter, it's a great crowd pleaser and stimulating entertainment.

Cycle-Cross: Cross country racing through the woods, streams, and paths, much like a massed start road race, with the winner the first rider to cross the finish line of the pre-determined course.

Bicycle Polo: Polo on bicycles instead of horses. Rarely seen in this country, as it requires big team efforts and specialized bicycles that can be used only for polo.

The ones to be dealt with are those the American athlete will encounter on the way to a Championship.

New York's Central Park Racing—Courtesy Howard Humphries

Control, Determination and Speed—Courtesy Milwaukee Sentinel

Time Trial Countdown—Courtesy Gene Portuesi's Cyclo-Pedia

Roller Racing—Courtesy Al Hatos

Cycle-Cross Racing—Courtesy Bicycle Institute of America

Prior to this, a general understanding has to be established. Let's begin with training. *Webster's 20th Century Dictionary of the English Language* defines "training" as:

1. The act of one who trains, educates or develops;
2. The state of being in good physical condition or fit;
3. Drill, manual exercises;
4. The training of the muscles and organs of the body by systematic exercise.

Whether you decide to try the road events or track events, the training to attain the Championship status must begin with a *complete* physical examination. *Not* the doctor's office pre-school $10.00 special, but a complete routine that most hospitals offer:

Blood Tests
Chest X-Ray
Cardiogram
Urinalysis

Plus a complete examination by a doctor who can give you an hour of his time for discussion. And, with what you're about to undertake, the doctor will be better able to evaluate any problems that need resolving *before* a program is begun. Certainly it's not worthwhile for me to say you might "have this or that," but I can give one example that's personal. It involved me. I am hypoglycemic. It took a five-hour blood study to determine this. Ask *any* doctor what can happen to a hypoglycemic athlete who is not aware of the necessary precautions.

This complete physical should be repeated annually. If I never convince anyone to compete, but have convinced them to have a thorough physical, I have achieved great success.

I just boil when I see parents expecting top performance from an athlete who has never even been routinely screened. Can you imagine a race car driver entering a car that has never been checked out?

Want some statistics? Out of 86 competitors or parents of competitors I contacted in Michigan in 1971, only 2 had received complete physical examinations (both of whom are my own personal friends). *All* the others had only the usual school examinations or none at all.

After the examination has been completed and you've resolved any difficulties, a few additional *don'ts* have to be fitted in:

1. Don't smoke.
2. Don't booze it up.
   And many *do's*.
1. Do try and keep regular hours.
2. Do try and get *at least* eight hours sleep.
3. Do establish a healthy diet program. Ask your doctor for a copy that will take into consideration the type of work load your body will be asked to provide. Don't have a food fetish. There's a need for all food groups, they work with each other in the body chemistry.

I also heartily recommend a copy of *Physiology of Exercise* by Laurence Morehouse and Augustus Miller. It's an excellent basis and reference source for actual body mechanics, that's updated at each printing.

General programming:

Children in racing: Before the meat of the program, a word about children in racing. They are *children*. Although the same basic principles apply for children as adults, the *child's* goals may be far different from what the parent expects. The child may just want the peer companionship or the identification grouping. Adults trend to project their own objectives as the child's. Therefore, small amounts of time to begin with—20 Minutes to 1/2 Hour daily are sufficient unless he's really competitive oriented. And if he (or she) doesn't like it, forget it!

Children in Racing, Midget Class—Courtesy Paul Gach

Getting with a good club and coach who can stimulate the child's interest is essential. Many times several neighborhood youths can be persuaded or interested in joining a club, and in this event, the chances of success are increased, and once they begin to "produce" the urge to overdo has to be firmly curbed.

Keep in mind that although our whole society is based on competition, it's hard to take defeat at any age, so whatever a child's performance, find something commendable.

Children in Racing, Intermediate Class—Courtesy Paul Gach

Adult programming: Begin a diary listing each day's routine, (work, school, cycling mileage). The time you spend cycling is only a part of your daily routine. If you work, sleep, eat, travel to and from work there are still other minor time consumers that are a part of your life.

Most begin their day at 7:30 and by the time you return home and get ready to cycle it's 6:00 p.m. or later. If you eat, it's usually 7:00 p.m. Now you can't begin at 7:00 p.m. and train 3 or more hours under these conditions. An hour and a half to 2 hours is all that can be managed. If you return home before dark, figuring dark at 9:00 or 9:30 p.m., it will be 10:00 before you have eaten, showered and fallen into bed. This gives you just 8 1/2 or 9 hours sleep, and you'll need all of it!

If you find yourself in different circumstances and can be a "sports bum" great, the program

can be expanded with workouts in both a.m. and p.m. 99% of us just don't fall in this group! One great lesson will be learned from this: the value of time.

1. List date, and weather conditions.
2. List how you feel, any particular stress you're under, any particular disability such as colds, fatigue, muscle aches, menstrual period, etc.
3. List type of exercises or training, and how much time is spent on each.
4. If you're doing times, list that day's temperature, humidity and wind direction and velocity, as well as the type of equipment and gears used.
5. Set a goal: State Championships, Nationals, Worlds. It's impossible to keep in peak condition all the time and bad psychologically. Decide what you're really going for, and use every other event leading up to this goal as a training exercise.

   No one ever remembers that I lost two or three races in the spring. They remember that I *won* National Championships and tied an existing World Record.
6. Understand that every training program has to have rest periods. If you find your weight going down and you're not trying for this, it could mean you're overtraining. This point is the hardest for the beginner to absorb because he's willing to go through hell's punishment to achieve. Muscles that aren't rested and ridding themselves of carbon dioxide can't develop or produce maximum energy.

   After completing the chapter you may have picked up enough enthusiasm to ride through a brick wall, but there's just no *easy* way to achieve and retain championship form. It's always hard work, requires complete regimentation, concentration, concentration on self and 100% devotion. There will be days when you certainly don't feel like exercising. OK, revise the schedule slightly, but unless you have a real physical problem, force yourself.

Women only: Menstruating is no reason to defer physical exercise unless your doctor feels you have a specific difficulty. I have never met one gal yet who was told to stay off the bicycle. Almost always the exercising will relieve any cramping in the lower abdominal region. Face reality, you can't pick your race dates according to your calendar. You race no matter what, so you'd better train with the same conviction.

The biggest problem most women run into is the pre-menstrual fatigue and depression. It generally is generated by the increased fluid in the system causing capillary pressure. How to relieve it? There are three accepted methods:

1. Go on a salt free diet ten days prior to your period.
2. Go on the salt free diet and have your gynecologist prescribe a dieuretic.
3. Have your gynecologist prescribe one of the special medications that are specifically designed to relieve extreme cases. For special competitive events the period can be delayed by one of the prescribed regulating drugs.

You might run into a problem with the dieuretic if you're planning on a 100 mile road race. In this event, skip the medication for that day. Keep in contact with your doctor, as there are always new medications coming on the market.

Sex and the single saddle: Whether you're male or female, discount any old wives tales that athletic activity decreases sexual stimulation. When the body is conditioned, *all* phases of activity improve. As a matter of fact and not conjecture, athletes are the horniest people around. Leaving all religious and moral conviction aside, young men and women I've consulted (both single and married) seem to feel there is nothing physically damaging by having intercourse the evening prior to the competitive event. It can promote a good night's sleep. However, if you plan to hunt up a partner a couple of hours prior to a meet with thought to improving your cycling performance, I'd forget it.

Psychology: Psychology has a far greater impact on the performance of an athlete than intercourse. It separates the good athletes from the champions. I've seen many physically superior riders fail every time with a victory in sight, while many non-championship calibre athletes defeat their opponents because they accepted the challenge instead of the question.

It's a hard thing to explain, other than calling it the killer instinct. I don't really like that term

because champion athletes are not uncaring egotists. They merely have the ability to size up a situation and take action. If you don't have it, you can't acquire it. All the training and conditioning possible can't make up for that split-second-hell-bent-for-leather decision when the pressure is on.

Massage: Massage can be a plus factor for the cyclist if the masseur knows his business . . . and the sport . . . and the cyclist. Just to say "I need a massage" isn't enough.

1. Is it for relaxation before an event?
2. Is it to counteract some specific muscle strain?
3. Is it to defatigue after competition?

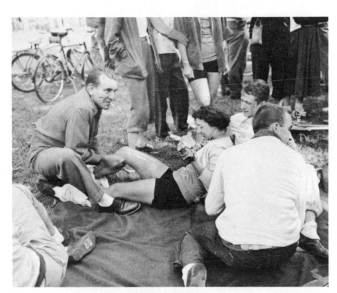

Pre–race massage—Courtesy Gene Portuesi's Cyclo-Pedia

All three are different, and require different technique. Most Americans, both male and female, have Victorian difficulty in stripping for a complete relaxation massage. My European experiences qualify me to say that all three are necessary at the championship level, on a regular basis. As a novice cyclist it's difficult to find a masseur, but there are a few self-relaxation massage techniques that can be managed. Since the legs are the prime source for fatigue and muscle strain it's this area that receives the most consideration. For a general relaxation massage after cycling, begin by:

A. Taking a warm relaxing bath.
B. Prepare for bed.

Olympic Coach Gene Portuesi, 1959 National Champion Joanne Speckin (Klein); and myself—Courtesy Gene Portuesi's Cyclo-Pedia

C. Once in bed, massage each individual leg in the following manner.

1. Legs slightly cocked in sitting position, begin by stroking from the top of the thigh down to the ankle in one long, soft stroke, about 25 times.
2. Gently, with the tips of the fingers, flip the calf muscles from side to side rapidly for about 30 seconds, moving up and down the area.
3. Repeat the flipping muscle action on the under-thigh for about 30 seconds.
4. Finish by stroking back from ankle to thigh about 25 times.

Repeat on other leg. Concentrate mentally on making the muscles and the whole body accept relaxation, almost a self-hypnosis state.

I might suggest a soft oil like Johnson's, or Dermassage as a lubricant for the massage. Pre-competition lubricant usually has some oil of winter-green to stimulate the skin and warmth, and isn't particularly suited to the spirit of bed-time!

Spring conditioning:

Fact! Bicycle racing is second only to sculling in stress and expending of energy, but the spring training *gently* begins after the holidays are over.

This section and most of what I know about cycling come through my personal contact with a man whom I consider the nation's finest cycling coach, Mr. Gene Portuesi. His reputation for developing champion cyclists brought him the well deserved honor of coaching the 1964 American Olympic Cycling Team in Japan, and will most certainly be reflected in my working with the women in the proposed 1980 Olympics in Russia.

To initiate conditioning, certain exercises must be used to strengthen. This happens when the muscle is required to contract to overcome a greater resistance and this request for energy strengthens the muscle. Jarring exercises that compress the skeletal structure are taboo. They cause strain on muscles and ligaments. Breathing exercises to expand the diaphragm also help increase the vital oxygen capacity in competition.

If you're overweight, get rid of it *now* by sound and steady dieting *before* the actual training season. This prevents exhaustion and fatigue from developing. You can't afford to cut down when the intensive energy output begins. Help this dietary program (medically prescribed) along by burning up calories on the road. This can be done by:

1. Put several layers of newspaper between wool sweaters, covering well both back and chest areas. Wool pants covered with another pair of stretchy materialed pants should finish the outfit.
2. Try and ride about 15 or 20 miles at a regular pace that will encourage perspiration. Concentrate on setting up action that will provide this without using any bursts of speed or sprinting. You don't want to strain anything, just sweat.

Change and shower immediately after the ride and crawl into bed if possible.

Early spring indoor training sessions should start with a calisthenic warm-up, four exercises, twenty repetitions. There are dozens of books on calisthenic and weight training. After you've read two, you'll be unable to get through a workout under five hours. That's why it's extremely important to pick those that are related to the cycling activity muscles.

Begin your initial session by measuring yourself, and recording change every six weeks. For instance, my own measurements at the beginning of a season were usually:

Neck—12 7/8"
Right Arm Bicep—10 1/2"
Left Arm Bicep—10 3/4"
Bust—38 1/2"
Midriff—30 1/2"
Waist—26"
Upper Hips at Hip Bone—29"
Lower Hips across Buttocks—36"
Right Thigh—22 3/4"
Left Thigh—22 1/4"
Right Knee—14 1/2"
Left Knee—14 1/2"
Right Calf—14 1/2"
Left Calf—14 1/4"
Right Ankle—8 3/4"
Left Ankle—8 1/2"
Vital Capacity—33" (For Vital Capacity, put the tape on the midriff, exhale, then inhale and measure.

Standing Side Benders—Courtesy Nick Baranet

Measure prior to the workout. Generally, the fatty areas such as the waist and hips will reduce after 3 or 4 weeks, and the other areas will gain. *Exercises:*

In doing calisthenic exercises or any weight training exercise (*not* weight lifting) the important things to learn are correct breathing and form. How much weight you can handle is not as important as how it is handled. I might suggest that an expert in weight training be asked to demonstrate for at least two training sessions. He can prevent injury as well as illustrating how to get the most out of each exercise.

Standing side benders—One set of twenty repetitions

Start: Stand erect, feet apart approximate width of shoulders, arms extended straight out from sides. Exhale and bend forward to touch left foot with right hand. Keep knees locked. Inhale and return to starting position, exhale and bend forward to touch right foot with left hand. Inhale and return to starting position. This is a four-count exercise.

Standing Bend Overs—One set of twenty repetitions

Start: Stand erect, feet apart approximate width of shoulders, hands on hips. Exhale and bend at waist letting head pull the torso down as far as possible. Keep knees locked. Bob once and inhale to return to starting position. This is a two count exercise.

Breathe as deeply as possible with mouth and nostrils. This helps accelerate lung action. These two exercises are designed to stretch and limber and prevent the ballet dancer pedal action seen in the novice cyclist.

Bend Over, Squat and Toe Raise—One set, twenty repetitions

Start: Stand erect, feet apart approximate width of shoulders, hands on hips. Exhale and bend at waist letting head pull the torso as far down as possible. Keep knees locked. Inhale and return to starting position. Exhale and squat with arms extending directly in front at shoulder height. Inhale and return to starting position with hands on hips. Exhale and rise on toes. Inhale and return to starting position. This is a six-count exercise.

Make sure that during the squat part of the exercise the feet remain directly parallel and flat footed. Also, on arising out of the squat, make sure both legs work equally to push up, and that the back is kept as straight as possible. This again is a limbering exercise with accent on calf and thigh development.

Standing Lateral Benders—One set of twenty repetitions

Start: Stand erect, feet apart approximate width of shoulders, hands at sides. Keeping back straight, exhale and bend sideways from waist to right. Let the right hand slide down the right leg as far as possible while keeping legs stiff. Bob up a few inches, press down again, inhale and return to starting position. Repeat same movement to the left side and continue to alternate. This is a two-count exercise.

This is a stretch exercise designed to limber midsection and back muscle tissue.

Be sure to rest two or three minutes between each of the warm-ups. Shaking the extremities in a relaxed, limber manner also helps to lessen muscle tension.

After the initial warm-up period the exercises should be completed as follows:

The weights listed are suggested as starting weights. Men can advance faster than women . . . and farther. But the idea is not to weight *lift,* but to weight *train.* Therefore, a good measure for how much weight to handle can be established by saying that you should be able to go through one set of ten repetitions with relative ease.

Upright Rowing—One set, ten repetitions—Weight 35 pounds.

Stand erect with hands apart approximate width of shoulders. Squat and firmly grasp the bar, palms down. Inhale, and stand erect with bar at extended arm length. Exhale. Inhale during the complete act of raising the bar close to the body and directly up under the chin. As the bar reaches the chin, the forearm should be parallel to the bar. Exhale and return the bar close to the body to the extended arm position. Remember to keep knees locked and body straight.

Toe Raises—One set of ten repetitions—Weight 100 pounds.

Toe Raise—Courtesy Nick Baranet

For this exercise it is best to use a rack that can hold the weight so the athlete can walk under and place the weight securely on the back of the shoulders.

Stand erect with the weight on the back of shoulders, hands grasping the bar to comfort, feet parallel and apart the approximate width of shoulders. A piece of 2 x 4 wood should be laid so that the heel can rest on the floor and the toe and pad area of the foot are on the 2 inch side of the board. Keeping the back and legs straight, rock forward and up into a toe raise on the 4 inch side of the wood. Inhale on the rise, exhale on the descent. Don't permit the feet to weave or wobble sideways.

Upright Rowing—Courtesy Nick Baranet

This is a tremendous calf definition exercise and excellent for lower leg and foot muscles.

Two-Handed Curl—One set of ten repetitions—Weight 25 pounds

Dead Lifts—Courtesy Nick Baranet

Two Handed Curl—Courtesy Nick Baranet

Squat to pick up weight, palms up. Stand erect, always using leg power to raise the body. Bar and arms at extended arm length. Keep the chest arched, back straight and elbows at sides. Inhale and flex the arms to lift the weight until the bar touches the upper chest in a curling motion, elbows at 45-degree angle when bar is under chin. Exhale and let the weight return to the hip area. Check to make sure the weight is controlled on the descent, so that full benefit of tension is obtained. This is an arm exercise, so be careful about hunching the body to help the weight up to the shoulders.

This set exercises the arm and upper shoulder muscles. Arm development is essential for positive control of the bicycle.

Dead Lifts—One set of ten repetitions—Weight 45 pounds

Squat to pick up weight, palms down. Stand erect with arms at extended hanging position. Carefully step up on platform about 15 inches high (a good solid milk crate is excellent) with

hands apart approximate width of shoulders and firmly grasping the bar in front of hips. Keeping knees locked, exhale and bend forward letting weight pull the body down as far as possible without losing balance. Bob once, inhale and return to starting position. Roll shoulders as though shrugging and continue repetitions.

This set is primarily designed to limber, strengthen and stretch the rear thigh and calf muscles, and particularly aid in controlling the flat footed pedal action.

Military Press—One set of ten repetitions—Weight 35 pounds

Squat to pick up weight, palms down. Stand erect with arms at extended hanging position. Inhale and raise bar in a reverse curl movement to chest position. Exhale. Keep body erect, inhale and press bar upward and slightly backward over the top of the head until arms are fully extended. Exhale and return bar to chest position. Control the bar on the descent so full benefit of tension is obtained. Don't pop the stomach muscles.

This set is designed for the powerful back muscles, and arm muscles. Women benefit a great deal from a press exercise.

Squats—One set of ten repetitions—Weight 40 pounds

Squats—Courtesy Nick Baranet

Use the rack to place the weight directly on the back of the shoulders. Stand erect with hands grasping the bar to comfort, feet parallel and apart approximate width of shoulders. Exhale on the beginning of descent, keeping the back as straight as possible. When completely squatted, inhale and using the legs only, begin ascent and return to starting position. Exhale and inhale deeply while doing a toe raise and then continue with the second repetition. Keep feet flat during squat and be sure that only the legs are used as jacks to raise and lower the torso. Refrain from using extreme weight in this exercise, 40 to 100 pounds should be the limit.

The squat is a power exercise to strengthen the legs, and the toe raise for definition of calf-thigh areas. It provides the strength for the powerful thrust and pull action of rotating cranks.

Prone Press—One set of ten repetitions—Weight 40 pounds

Recline on a bench under the rack. Firmly grasp the bar with hands apart approximate width of shoulders. Arms parallel, palms up. Inhale, lift weight off the rack, exhale, let the bar descend until it touches the chest area, but not resting on the chest. Inhale and push the weight up until the arms are fully extended. Continue repeti-

tions. The bench should be narrow enough to allow the shoulders to work freely.

This is an arm, back and chest exercise and provides the muscle power that is necessary for pulling on the bars during exerting energy outputs.

Bent Over Rowing—One set of ten repetitions—Weight 40 pounds

This is relatively the same as upright rowing only in a bent over position with head resting on a high stool. Hands should grasp the bar approximate width of shoulders, palms down. Inhale and stand with weight at extended arm's length. Exhale and bend over letting the bar swing forward until it is below the chest area. Inhale and raise bar up to chest, exhale and let bar descend until arms are extended again. Continue repetitions with head remaining on stool for the full ten repetitions.

This is primarily a pull exercise, designed to strengthen the muscles that control the handlebars, (back, chest and arms).

After these eight weight exercises, continue with sit-ups.

Sit-ups—Two sets of ten repetitions

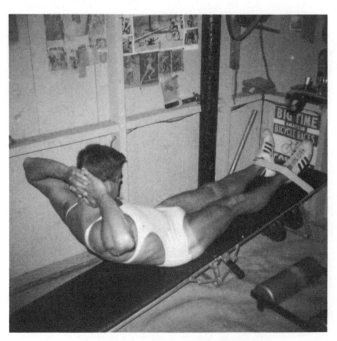

Sit-ups—Courtesy Nick Baranet

Lie on back on an inclined board with head down, feet up. Lock hands behind head by holding a stick to prevent elbow flap. Hook feet through a restraining strap or have someone hold the ankles firmly. Inhale and sit up, exhale and return to prone position.

An excellent exercise to tighten abdominals.

After completing the workout, ride rollers for about 5 to 10 minutes. It's the one exercise that emphasizes lung action and pedalling techniques, and sprinting (riding as fast as possible) permits a feeling of all-out spinning action.

Begin by rotating the cranks at about 100 or 110 r.p.m. for 3 or 4 minutes. Slow down for about another minute (90 r.p.m.s) then attempt an all out sprint for one minute. The novice usually manages 130 or 135 r.p.m.'s. The experienced cyclist, 165 or 170. I never knew anyone who broke 200; my own was around 180. After the sprint ride slowly for 3 or 4 minutes to cool down. It's exhausting, and yet very stimulating.

Shower and change clothes. Nothing is worse than the clammy chill of damp clothing.

That ends the indoor workouts.

As soon as the warm weather breaks, forget all but three of the weight exercises: The Military Press; the Dead Lift; the Curls. Never increase the weight once the road work has started, but keep at the same medium weights. Remember to continue the warm-ups *before* each ride, adding the sit-ups as a pre-riding exercise. Pulled or strained muscles are avoided by these exercises.

A schedule for the first three months might be:

Monday—If the weather permits, a low gear ride at an easy pace. If not, the complete workout.

Tuesday—If the weather permits, a low gear ride at a brisk pace, about 1/2 hour. If not, the complete workout.

Wednesday—The complete workout.

Thursday—If the weather permits, a low gear ride at an easy pace. If not, the complete workout.

Friday—Rest Day

Saturday—If the weather permits, a low gear ride at an easy pace. If not the complete workout.

Sunday—If the weather permits, a low gear ride at a brisk pace for 1 1/2 to 2 hours. If not, a good walk for the same time period, with calisthenics *only* prior to the walk.

Note: If the weather is good enough to ride outside, remember to complete the calisthenic part of the workout prior to the ride.

The gears should be restricted to 60 to 64 inches; they develop cadence.

If you run into a problem of scheduling, rotate the rest day.

Don't hang around talking after the workout. Change clothes and shower. Damp clothing chills, chills initiate muscle spasms and colds, colds circumvent all training.

Cycling Season:

Once the warm weather has arrived, all effort should be dedicated toward riding. The scheduling might go as follows for April.

Monday—Calisthenics and low gear ride (60 to 64 inch gear) at an easy pace for at least 20 miles.

Tuesday—Calisthenics and 3 Weight Training Exercises first. Low gear ride at a brisk pace for about 10 miles.

Wednesday—Calisthenics and track (velodrome) workout on a medium gear (68 to 72 inches). Approximately an hour of actual riding time should be completed.

Thursday—Calisthenics and 3 Weight Training Exercises first. Low gear ride at easy pace for about 20 miles.

Friday—Rest Day

Saturday—Calisthenics and track (velodrome) workout on a medium gear (68 to 72 inches). Approximately an hour of actual riding time should be completed.

Sunday—Calisthenics and road ride of at least 50 miles in April, 70 in May and 90 in June. Ride at a good pace without tincanning.

Remember to rotate the rest day. Many times Monday will be the alternative after the Sunday siege.

Once the racing season is really going (May, June, etc.), Sundays are always race dates and Monday is many times the date for that *needed* rest. Don't just limit yourself to one day if you feel you really need it. Gears should increase as cadence develops. However, keep one day a week as a low gear day to retain action. The actual racing gear you will use will be determined by your times and performance.

Specializing:

Today is the day of the specialist. It's impossible to be a road racer, sprinter, 1000 M Time Trialist or Pursuitist all rolled up in one neat package. The fine training for each is different. The strategy is different. The racing is different. But each of these specialist categories is fitted into the overall training program by initiating the specific training methods on the Wednesday, Saturday and Sunday schedules.

Track Racing—Sprinting:

The development of a good track rider will naturally begin with the road work in the spring scheduling. Once the track season has opened the track events are fitted into the schedule.

Sprinting is designed to develop maximum speed, and in order to initiate the sprint, the "Jump" has to be developed. "Jumping" is the initial burst of speed to propel the bike into the sprint. Without a "jump" the fastest rider in the world couldn't get out of his own way.

Jumping is the prime winner of sprinting races and can't be practiced enough. The action of a jump is to pull the body forward off the saddle with the arms and push down and *pull up* on the pedals as hard as possible—in one smooth effort. The bars should not be used just as a place to rest the arms, but to pull the body and legs in a tremendous burst.

Initiating a jump—Courtesy Paul Gach

One action that is never emphasized enough for sprinters is the "pull up" pedal action in the jump. Pushing on the pedals is only half the energy force available, while one leg is pushing, the other must be pulling. This is the main reason for toe clips and straps and the flat pedal action.

Occasionally a rider with extremely poor pedal action might be required to remove one crank of the free-wheeling road bicycle and propel the cycle by using the one leg. This is a sure-fire method of developing the "pull-up"; you have to or you fall off the bicycle.

The jump itself should only last for ten or twelve complete revolutions of the crank. After this initial burst, the rider should reseat himself in a smooth effort and continue to apply full power of the legs from the fulcrum of the saddle. This reseating has to be one smooth action, to keep power in the stroke and not break stride. It is impossible to keep the smooth action if the rear is just "plunked" back on the saddle.

Once the jump has been initiated, how far you can extend yourself flat out is the next question.

Fact: The human body can extend itself at an all-out power effort for twelve to fourteen seconds. This is the fact that necessitates each individual to determine his own best jumping distance.

Example: From my own training journal—

Gear 82, Wind 4 m.p.h. cross, flat surface

Initiating my jump at 250 yards—my time was 14.8
Initiating my jump at 240 yards—my time was 14.6
Initiating my jump at 230 yards—my time was 14.4
Initiating my jump at 220 yards—my time was 14.4
Initiating my jump at 210 yards—my time was 16.0
Initiating my jump at 200 yards—my time was 16.0

By a check of the times, consistently, my best distance to initiate a sprint if I was controlling the race was 230 yards. If the field was already flying (maybe 28 m.p.h.) it would be impractical to initiate my sprint from 230, as a good amount of energy is already being expended. However, if the field moves at 18 m.p.h. and it's possible to initiate the sprint from 230 yards with a blasting jump, chances there isn't anybody going by. Check your cadence. If you can't spin the gear, don't use it.

If the field is moving at a speed great enough to nullify the jump, pick the best wheel, sit on for the lovely windbreak, and then bomb by at least 50 yards prior to the finish. You can't afford

A well planned finish—Courtesy Al Hatos

to let the field get to top speed and just sit on, however. Why? Because most likely any top notch athlete against whom you compete has a speed that is equal to yours. The jump is what opens up a gap between riders and the "kick" or "on the saddle second jump" 50 yards from the finish line keeps the field from passing. This is true if you're sprinting on the road or riding track races.

An important point to discuss is windbreak advantage. The front riders in a fast moving field cut the wind friction for the following riders by as much as 25%. This is saved energy for these riders who can use it in their "jumps" or "kicks" at the finish line. The rider who is sitting in the middle of a little group is really coasting along.

A disadvantage to this "protected" rider occurs when action takes place on the fringe of the pack and the middle rider is "boxed" and can't move out to become a part of the action. Seasoned riders learn how to take advantage of windbreak without putting themselves at a disadvantage.

Open track racing: Midgets, Intermediates, Juniors generally ride the open track race, but occasionally Seniors and Women may have this race as an added feature. It's merely each class of riders going for a certain number of laps with the first man across the line at the finish declared the winner. Here again the "jump" is used on the last lap to obtain top speed.

Sprint racing: is the really classical phase of track racing. It's a part of our State, National, Olympic, Pan American and World Championships.

In the qualifying rounds there may be 3 riders paired together, in the semi-finals and finals only 2 go together. The distance is anywhere from 500 to 1000 Meters depending on the track size.

When the competitor reaches the semi-finals in sprint racing, he can be sure again that his competitor is every bit as fast. So, how to win? Tactical Maneuvering! Example: The gun goes

Open Track Racing—Courtesy Al Hatos

off at the start. The riders very slowly leave the starting line. One of the two goes up front (eventually) the other stays behind this front rider. Occasionally, both riders effect surplace (staying in a fixed position) by angling the front wheel up the track banking and balancing. This is done when neither rider wants to start off. It's a killer on both nerves and muscles but can effect a great psychological defeat to the man who finally is forced to move out.

Some riders like the front position, some like the rear. Some do both, but generally there's a preference for position. If both riders like the front position there will be many cuttings up and down the track, many quick jumps to try and obtain the front position, and some very stimulating racing. Those who prefer the front position claim:

A. They feel they have complete control of the match.

B. The fact they're one bike length ahead already is advantageous in their jump.

C. He has the possibility of initiating the sprint, going only 3/4 full, and then blasting again when the opponent attempts to come around.

Those who prefer the rear state:

A. They aren't forced to keep watching to the rear to observe their opponent. This can be pretty nerve wracking if the 2d rider falls a bike length or so back of the lead rider.

B. This half hidden positioning permits greater surprise.

Regardless of who prefers what, the object is to outmaneuver, place the opponent at a disadvantage, or minimize his potential. This might be "boxing" the opponent by forcing your opponent between you and the top of the bicycle velodrome. He is then forced to back off, try and swing down the track to reposition himself. You in turn accelerate, keeping him in back of you, and force him down to the bottom. It's vicious, it's explosive, it requires that split-second-timing called "killer instinct."

If you make a mistake in the early qualifying rounds and fail to qualify you can come back through a "repecharge" (another chance). But in the semi-finals, there's only ONE chance. The finals have riders for 1st and 2nd riding the best of three races, and riders for 3rd and 4th riding the best of three races.

Each heat (qualifying race) is different, each rider enters the race with a complete tactical plan that might have to be changed after the first 50 meters. But when you are in top competition watch your competitors. They have patterns. They will rely on these patterns, and you can defeat them because of this. (Of course the same will be true of you.)

Warm–ups–Courtesy Paul Gach

Great Form!–Courtesy Paul Gach

You can help defeat them psychologically as well, before the race. Always look sharp. Walk on the velodrome infield with confidence. Have a routine pattern set-up for equipment stationing. Have your masseur give a slight relaxing rub after you've taken off your track suit. Sit and rest comfortably. DON'T walk around obviously checking out your competition. Ride your rollers 2 or 3 minutes prior to your event. Walk with confidence up to the line with your trainer. You might specifically ask your trainer for a drink from your water bottle just prior to mounting the bicycle. Even though you don't have to drink and it might just be water. . . . it drives your competition up a wall to know just what you've got that makes you go faster! Above all, don't fraternize. You're there to compete, not socialize. All these bits of "needling" are worthless if you finish in last place.

A word about sportsmanship. In any competition there are little nasty maneuvers that can create unpleasantness. I mention them only because top notchers don't need to resort to these for a victory!

To practice and get into that "big league" competition requires constant riding situations at the velodrome. With every session you learn, as well as refining your physical conditioning.

Don't forget the warm-ups, then before the actual tracing sessions plan a group warm-up. Ask 5 or 6 riders to form a chain (one rider behind the other). Each rider takes a certain distance at the front of the field, and then falls back to the rear, the next man taking his turn at the front, etc. The distance for each rider to head the field can be 1/2 lap of the track or maybe 3/4 of a lap. At the beginning, the pace is moderate, then it speeds up to a final fast finish, maybe even a sprint, taking about 20 minutes for completion. After this warm-up period rest a short time. Then begin practicing *jumps* or *actual track competition.*

Under actual racing conditions, it might be impossible to warm-up before you're called to the line. This is another reason to own a set of rollers. A five minute easy warm-up will relax all the track tension, and loosen nerved-up muscles. This warm-up is good for any type of track or road event you'd ride. Roller warm-ups can be substituted prior to a road race if the rider just doesn't have the time to put in 2 or 3 miles of road warm-up.

What gears to ride? As stated in the touring section, cadence is the answer. If you can't consistently rotate a gear at about 100 r.p.m.s, it's too high. If you're sprinting that gear should be able to be rotated over 110. Times, plus cadence should equal the best gear for the rider. This changes as the physical conditioning improves, but the greatest hazard is to overgear. The attitude of riding the gear that the National Champion rides is hard to overcome in the novice.

An additional notation that should be observed is that sprinting is extremely strenuous. Don't plan on doing 15 or 20 a session. Try for 4 or 5 at first, and be prepared for an occasional reaction (regurgitating) until you're accustomed to sprinting. *Tandem Sprinting*—This operates on the same principles of individual sprint racing, except a tandem with two riders is used. Track maneuvering is relatively the same, the jump is the same, but the top speeds are faster. It's a glorifying race to watch, exhilarating and exciting. A top notch tandem team should be pretty evenly matched physically and jump wise; but two good sprinters can give a championship performance occasionally without ever having practiced over long periods. Although not ridden in the State and National Championships, Tandem Racing is generally done in the Worlds, Olympic and Pan American contests.

Pursuit—Another phase of track racing. Just like it sounds, somebody chasing somebody else. Gen-

Champion Nancy Burghart warming up—Courtesy Nick Baranet

Tandem Tension—Courtesy Nick Baranet

erally it's two people, occasionally, it's more.

Two man pursuit is the one I'm primarily concerned with because it's another event that gets a rider into the State, National Olympic, Pan American and World Championships.

Training for this event is entirely different than training for the classical sprinting. The psychological make-up of the pursuiting athlete is many times different from that of the sprinter.

It doesn't always take that "killer instinct." It takes something else, perhaps even more, it takes the ability to *suffer*, *to persevere*, *to endure*, something the true sprinter can never achieve.

Distance for men is 4000 Meters and women, 3000 Meters.

Here again the specialization takes over. Just how do you ride 4000 meters? Phase one is to set yourself a goal.

Example: You are going to do a 4000 Meter Pursuit. In order to make the finals you will have to do a near record ride the first time. You know what the record is, but in April, you're not going

"Go!"—Champion John Vande Velde—Courtesy Bill Olsen

for that record. You're going for that record in August. So, in April you'll set yourself a goal in an Interval Training Schedule.

What is an Interval Training Schedule? It's doing two or three laps at a time, and attempting to turn out specific lap times down to the second for each lap. For instance (I'm rounding out the laps to even seconds so it's easier to understand) if a record time for 4000 Meters is 5 minutes flat, and it takes 10 laps of your track to equal 4000 meters, your time for each lap must approximate 30 seconds a lap.

Now this is not quite accurate because your first lap will be off approximately 5 seconds or so because the starting lap is the slowest. So you would probably figure 35 seconds for the first lap and 29 seconds for each of the following 9 laps, rounding out the time to 4 minutes and 56 seconds.

In April you might want to settle for a 6 minute time:

1st Lap—40 seconds

2nd through 10th laps—35 seconds

making a time of 5 minutes and 55 seconds.

Now you have the formula. How to develop those 35 second laps is the next step of the interval training. You must have someone there to time you. After a warm-up and short rest, remount the bicycle with the thought in mind that you are going to do 35 second laps no faster, no slower. Ride 2 laps at an easy pace, then ride 2 or 3 attempting to maintain 35 seconds. It won't take long to feel the rhythm and breathing necessary to maintain the 35 seconds. After the timed laps, ride two more easy, then do another 2 or 3 timed laps. Continue this pattern for about an hour. That's a real workout for both you and your timer!

Once a week or every 10 days try a full 4000. Remember that you are not going for a record, merely the 35 second lap times.

As the season progresses, your gearing will go up (remember about cadence—if you can't spin it, don't use it) and your lap times will have to be readjusted, because through conditioning, your times will be improving. Continue the interval training with reduction of seconds per lap until you have reached your goal. Of course, you may

not reach your goal, and may have to settle for what is reality in how fast you *can* do the distance. There's always next year!

The timer is an important part of developing the pursuitist. He has to be familiar with you, as well as competently able to time. When you are attempting a full 4000 meters it is up to him to keep you posted on your progress. When you start your 4000 he will be stationed at one particular spot on the track you have picked and have your schedule in hand worked out in full timing. *Example:* Take the 5:55 timing that has 40 seconds for the first lap, 35 seconds for each additional lap.

1st Lap	40 Seconds
2nd Lap	1 Minute 15 Seconds
3rd Lap	1 Minute 50 Seconds
4th Lap	2 Minutes 25 Seconds
5th Lap	3 Minutes
6th Lap	3 Minutes 35 Seconds
7th Lap	4 Minutes 10 Seconds
8th Lap	4 Minutes 45 Seconds
9th Lap	5 Minutes 20 Seconds
10th Lap	5 Minutes 55 Seconds

This scheduling will change with each track you ride on because of the varying distances of the individual tracks. But it's extremely easy to set up a schedule once you know how many laps make the 4000 meters. 95% of the tracks are either 1/4 or 1/5th mile in length.

Now, it is impossible for the timer to yell your time to you every time you come by, and it's also confusing. What he has to yell at you is a choice of three things:

1. ON (Meaning you're right on the time you've set.)

2. 1 UP (Meaning you're one second ahead of what you've scheduled.)

3. 1 DOWN (Meaning you're one second behind what you've scheduled.)

If you're UP, ease it a little. If you're DOWN, pick it up a little. Sounds simple, but for the rider who is out there straining, it's hell. When you've consistently scheduled a time that finds you down 2, 4, 6, 8 seconds a lap, etc., it's going to take more interval training to get the feeling of getting those stable laps.

After the qualifying rounds have selected the

finalists for pursuit (and these rounds are always judged by the fastest times) the final rounds are actual pure pursuit. . . . with one rider trying to keep ahead of his opponent. I would feel free in saying that most pursuitists still attempt to do a scheduled ride unless they really know their competition's weak points.

I can give an example of this. At one National Championship where I officiated, the 1st and 2nd riders came to the line. The first rider was aware of the fact that the second rider couldn't stand to be behind during the initial 3 or 4 laps, so he deliberately set out to go harder than he normally would the first 4 laps. It blew #2's mind! When he had completed his 1st lap and looked across the track to his opponent, he saw he was almost 4 bike lengths down (behind). You could see

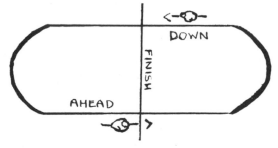

Down—In a pursuit

him hunch and dig-in because he felt he had to immediately recover the 4 lengths by the next lap. What happened next was natural. He had completely lost his sense of timing, and died (exhausted himself mentally and physically) during the 6th lap. Now #1 rider's final time was way off the record already established that day by almost 12 seconds, but he had defeated his competition, and that was his goal!

Australian Pursuit—Another form of pursuit, but not a championship event. It can have up to 8 riders beginning at different equally spaced parts of the velodrome. As a rider is caught by the one behind, he is eliminated. It can be for a set number of laps or set time.

Italian Pursuit—Again pursuit, but non-championship. It can have 2 or more teams of 3 to 5 riders starting at equally spaced parts of the velodrome. If there are 5 riders per team, the race is 5 laps

long, with each of the riders doing one lap and then going off the track. The race is then decided by the time of the last man in each team as he finishes. This is a fast, but exciting spectator event.

Harness Pursuits—Again pursuit, but non-championship. This event lets 2 or 3 riders form a team and each team's members can take turns pacing each other. Winning team is judged by the fastest time for a specific number of laps.

1000 Meter Time Trial—A State, National, Pan American and Olympic event held on the track. Just as it sounds, it is a time trial for 1000 Meters. The rider is held for balance by a starter. On the "go" signal he must propel the bicycle from this standing start as fast as he can, for the distance. It is a single competitor event and probably as physically devastating as pursuit. The initial surge

Champion Jack Simes III—Courtesy Al Hatos

of power to get the bicycle to the rider's top speed has to be smooth and powerful. It can't be the kind of all out sprinter jump that lasts for 300 yards, it has to be a building acceleration and then a sustained time trial effort.

Here again, getting the feel of "almost full out" laps has to be developed and timing with the Interval Training Method can be the key to success. It's my feeling that the accent should be on the power acceleration. If it's too fast the rider is "burned out," if it's too slow, time is lost. Again, gearing restrictions are governed by cadence: if you can't spin it, don't use it.

10 Mile Open—I mention this specifically, because it's one event that is a National Championship event for the men and yet it does not appear in the Olympics, Pan American Games or World Championships. It's really a massed start race on the track, with up to 40 or more riders, depending on track size. All the riders start together and are given one lap to organize the field. The second lap finds every man for himself and each jamming to drop the less astute. All lapped riders are called out of the race. The constant jumping and jamming very quickly reduced the field to only the very hearty. If there ever was a place to visualize what happens in road racing, the 10 miler gives a capsule view. Most of these races are ridden at 30 plus m.p.h.

Ten Miler Line-up—Courtesy Paul Gach

Although it is a test of supreme strength and stamina, it is almost always won by a sprinter, but it's never a "give away" victory.

Point Race is another track event in which a group of riders from 5 to 30 sprint each lap for points. First place can be given 5 points, 2nd place 3 points, 3rd place 1 point. The final lap might even award double points (10 for 1st, 6 for 2nd, 2 for 3rd.) Winner is determined by the man with the greatest number of points. It's a visually exciting race but very difficult for the spectators to evaluate, because it requires constantly applying points to the individual riders as they accrue.

Madison is the only contribution America has made toward establishing a specific event in cycle racing. It comes from Madison Square Garden where the 6-day first achieved great popularity at the turn of the century. It's vivid, it's exciting,

Alf Goullet, Newark Velodrome Star—Courtesy Otto Eisele

it's physically strenuous, and many times somewhat hazardous, but it's always a crowd pleaser.

Basically, it's a race between teams consisting of two riders who may relieve each other at any time (except during the sprints, primes, or final lap). One rider is always riding hard, while the other rests, then the resting rider swings down into the field of action letting his partner "throw" him into the fast travelling field. The rider who has just finished a hard ride then swings up to the top of the track where he rides slowly around until it is his turn to get back in the action.

The changing usually is predetermined by the two team mates, perhaps every second or third lap, or every two and a half laps. It depends on the size of the track.

The "throw" is usually accomplished with the retiring rider catching his teammate by a tool taped in the left side of his tights and then using his arm, body force and speed, hurl the teammate into the action.

"Throw"—Courtesy Otto Eisele

The length of the race is usually determined by time (1 hour is very popular) rather than distance, with points scored every number of set laps. The object is really to gain a lap on the other teams, but if no one manages to gain a lap on the other teams, the team with the greatest number of points is declared the winner.

It sounds simple, but to me it's extremely hazardous and requires fantastic bicycle handling to zip in and around, and up and down the track while 8 or 10 teams are jamming hard and changing partners at the same time. As a matter of fact, I've seen some wicked spills by inexperienced track men. Ideally, the perfect team

should consist of a real sprinter who comes in just prior to the sprint, and a pursuitist type who can suffer at sustained high speeds. It's not a championship event, merely a spectator sport, and many of the top riders who are training for a goal refuse to get involved.

Devil Take-the-Hindmost (Miss and out) Another track event very popular with the spectators. The race starts with any number of riders, from 10 to 30. Every time they pass the finish line the last man over the line is called out of the race. This is usually carried down until there are 3 men left, and then those 3 sprint the final lap for final positioning.

"No. 4, you're out!"—Courtesy Paul Gach

Road Racing—Massed Start

Massed Start road racing is really the oldest form of competition in the bicycle's history. Long before velodromes were invented, the town boys were trying to out-do one another around the country square.

In Europe it has always been the "going thing," with the Tour de France holding the same position as the World Series of Baseball. It's a very strong and exciting event for the men, but never caught on as a women's event. French promoters attempted to stimulate interest and did run an international women's event, but it didn't succeed. Apparently Frenchmen still feel a woman belongs in bed and not on a bicycle.

Now, the large men's road racing events are suffering. As the automobile traffic increases, the

Roadrace at Rahway, New Jersey—Courtesy Al Hatos

amount of road racing decreases. In the United States where the automobile is supreme, it's a great experience to see one hundred or more cyclists charging down a road with flashing spokes and rainbowed jerseys, led by a blaring police car . . . and followed by an entourage of screaming supporters hanging out of cars in the following motorcade.

Because of the tremendous amount of logistics involved in this type of road race, the most common event is the Circuit Race. It can be easily controlled and attracts spectators. The circuit can be around a small town, a plaza parking lot, a park or anywhere there's a good circular type course.

If the race is called a Criterium, it's generally under 50 miles, and might even have several sprints for points called for.

If it's over 50, it's considered an Open Road

Race. The amount of miles for each Rider Class is specified in the Amateur Bicycle League of America Handbook.

Champion Jack Heid winning Tour of Somerville, N.J.—Courtesy Al Hatos

The season varies with each section of the country. In California they begin in February, in the Midwest and East in late March. Yet it's difficult to say that because the west coast riders have a longer time to train, they're better road men. They aren't. It's always been the individual effort that's developed the Champion.

The training for the extended road races, if fitted into the overall training program listed previously, with the track events being deleted and the longer road rides put in their place, is complete.

Roads and courses will vary with each part of the country, and with the National Championships in any part of the United States, a rider has to be prepared for extreme mountain ranges, as well as the Midwest flats.

In most massed start racing, the best riders set the pace hard as soon as the race has begun. The main reason for this is because the novice can be more readily disposed of, there is less chance for accident with less astute bike riders out of the field, and it gets rid of the sprinters who many times bury themselves in the field until 300 yards before the finish. An aggressive cyclist will always attempt to blow the field apart right at the start. But it won't succeed if he's alone in this effort. A group travelling together is at least 5 to 6 m.p.h. faster than an individual. So any attack has to be supported, and generally riders from a club or area, and in some cases just 4 or 5 riders from anywhere to work together.

Remember the windbreak faction? The leader is expending far more energy than those "sitting on his wheel." So, if three of the group plan to attack, they will jump together and then take turns at the head of the three man peleton (organized group). If one of the three tried to pull the other group of two he wouldn't last more than a mile or two before he was completely exhausted. Champions keep a reserve for the final sprint.

I contend there are three ways to ride a road race:
1. Attack and try to break from the group.
2. Sit in the field and hope no breaks get away.
3. Ride at the head of the field and try to maintain a high, but steady pace. This pretty much nullifies outside attack.

1. *Attack:* Just like it sounds. A group (4 or 5) of riders agrees to attempt a break from the field. They can manage this in a number of ways.
A. The whole group of five casually ride up at the front of the pack. The first three pull a 3/4 out jump to pull away from the front of the field. The 4 and 5th rider, remain at the head of the pack and make a very half-hearted attempt to chase. They will fall into the chasing peleton (organized group), and as each man takes his turn to head the group, he would ease the pace slightly. This has to be done very craftily because it doesn't take long for the real chasers to figure out "who is on whose side," and make sure that a real chaser is always heading the field. Another factor to be considered is "where" the attempted break should take place. Certainly, the best place is not on nice flat straight roads. It's in the curvy, hilly, terrain where the field itself is busy doing its best to stay together and is not watching for breaks. Remember, that once that gap is opened from the departing attack group it provides that buffeting wind factor that psychologically defeats the chasing group.

Where to pull this break in relation to the distance of the race is arbitrary. If you break shortly after the start, the small break away group has to rely on themselves over a mighty long course, and the chasing field can usually muster 8 to 10 really good riders who will try and bring them back into the pack.

If you wait to the end of the race the field is wary and any group is seldom let away because everybody is watching.

I feel that the best time should be governed by the terrain, and probably from the first third to half of the distance.

There are those who "go" right from the start, and the psychological impact of this is certainly in their favor. So you "pays your money and takes your choice."

If the first attack fails, another attack should be launched almost immediately,

Sigfried Koch attempting a road break—Courtesy Paul Gach

with the sequence of riders changing places, *i.e.*, two of the break group now stay at the head of the pack, and the two who were at the head of the pack go with the other teammate to attack. And on, until the successful break is established.

The break itself can be made from the front of the field, as I've stated, or from the side of the near front of the grouped field—never from the rear if the pack is large. Why? Because by the time the attacking group has reached the front of the field every rider passed will know what you're attempting. Also, those in the rear will be

shouting to let those up front know that a break is being attempted. When you go from the near front, the riders in the middle and rear of the pack might not even know you've gotten away. I've even seen races where those in a grouped sprint for the finish didn't know there were four or more men away who had already crossed the finish line. Keep sharp and don't get involved in distracting conversation.

When you plan the attack, either attack from the front, or near front outside—never from inside the field. All it takes to wipe out your effort would be for someone to ride in front of you. Stay away from road edges as there's a greater tendency toward puncturing.

When you initiate your *outside* attack jump 3/4 out and aim to ride the closest safe line to the riders you are by-passing.

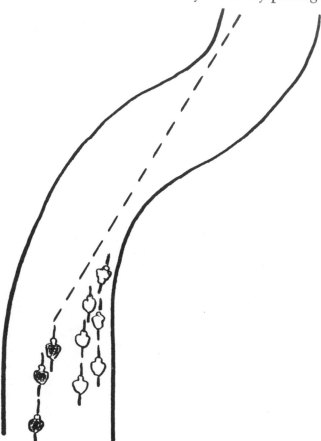

Breakaway strategy

It limits their room to maneuver, and gives an impression of terrific speed.

Gear up to your best cadence gear, or down to it if you've been sitting in the middle of the field coasting with a "goliath" gear. Make sure your toe clips and straps are tight. Hyperventilate. But don't broadcast it obviously. Anybody watching knows the signs of preparation.

Once you're physically and psychologically set, initiate your jump—not the sprinter's full-out jump. It can be the "on the saddle" kick type of jump, or a "3/4 out" off the saddle jump. If you were to jump fullforce like the sprinters your jump would last how far? 300 Yards! Unfortunately you still have 75 miles to go.

The thrust should get you out of the 20

plus field speed, up to the higher 28 to 30 m.p.h. that you hope to sustain. But the break, the separating the field is the advantage you've obtained.

Don't bother to look back immediately. You can pretty much tell by listening whether you've dragged half the field with you. Check after about 30 seconds. If there's a split, you've got a chance. If you're on a curvy road it's even better because "out of sight, out of mind!"

Now is the time to begin that "time trialing" attack, although your initial thrust speed will have eased. Each rider should take a turn at the front for about 200 meters, the units have to work as a whole. To keep pace from slacking the leader speeds up slightly before pulling to the side to let the next rider assume the leader position. Effort should progressively increase until it's maximum and sustained.

When the successful break comes close to the finish line, most riders will then attempt another individual break, or some advantageous move to win them the race. This is understood before, or settled during the race. It's natural for the best time-trialer to know he can get only 3rd place if the 2 with him are good sprinters. So he will attempt to get away by himself before the end. In return, the 2 sprinters will know this is going to happen so they'll be watching. Many times the group within itself will say "nobody makes a break before the final 1/2 mile mark. Whatever is decided, know what the finish area looks like and just what point to begin the sprint.

A word about "individual" attempts to break from the field early in a race. It's hardly ever successful if it's a quality field. One man cannot go as fast as a combined group. It might succeed if the group really doesn't think he stands a chance and doesn't bother to chase. But forget it if there's a headwind.

Speaking of wind, a word about how to get the best advantage if there's a strong wind. The best way to explain this is with illustrations. If there's a head wind, the riders should follow wheel to wheel directly beside each other without overlapping.

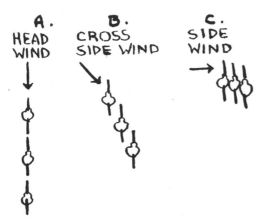

A., B., C., Wind resistance strategy

If there's a slight side wind, mostly head wind, the riders observe this pattern.

And, if it's an altogether side wind, this pattern.

Use any condition to your own advantage that's safe. If you hear riders talking, they're expending energy, a good time to attack. If they're tightening straps, feeding, changing gears, some particular road obstruction, railroad crossings, a flat tire or even a crash.

Sometimes overtaking traffic provides a terrific windbreak which can be used to initiate an attack. Although the rider is forbidden to take pace from vehicles, the side draft is energy.

If you're passing a group of riders, pass as close to them as safely possible so they will not be able to slip-stream quickly and move into your own little group.

Once the finish line is in sight, the same tactics that govern sprinting on the track, govern sprinting on the road. You can't go too soon, or you'll die before the finish line. You can't afford to sit in the sprinting group 50 yards from the finish, you have to "kick" out. You have to know your opposition as to whose wheel will pull you in closest to the finish line so you can initiate your own sprint.

In the big league racing, team effort has

already established who will lead out the sprint for the team's strongest sprinter to take advantage of by sitting behind that rider tightly. The Russians, Italians and French are great at this. Two know they are going to be sacrificed. The National victory is the prize. Americans are too greedy. I really shouldn't say that because we are seldom around for the finish of Pan American, Olympic or World Championship Road Racing Massed Start events, (excepting Mrs. Audrey McElmury, who won her gold medal victory at Brno, Czechoslovakia, 1969, in a one-man break-away shortly before the finish of the event and John Howard, who scored a Pan American victory by winning the 1971 Road Race in Cali, Colombia).

Basically, the Europeans are nearly professionals with their teams picked way in advance of actual events. They train together, eat, sleep and think together and they do without fail whatever their coach tells them.

American teams are picked two to three weeks prior to their competitive events. Each training method may differ from the next mans, and each thinks his training method and style of riding is the ultimate. To cohesively orient a team like this is impossible. The coach is forever forced to hear "lip" from this assembled multitude. If our riders were a little hungrier, or given the European system of supporting an athlete, our progress would advance significantly.

2. *Sit In*—The sit in the field and hope no breaks get away was my style of racing on the continent. And many sprinters score victories this way. But in the big league, where riders know each other the probability of this happening is minimal.

The only sprint I ever made in the stage racing came because there were no breaks. I took second place (Criterium Cycliste Feminin Lyonnaise-Auvergne, 5th Stage at Roanne, France) but was beaten anyway by Millie Robinson on her 110″ gear.

Champion Jack Simes winning Tour of Somerville, N.J.—Courtesy Al Hatos

3. *Riding at the head of the field*—Defensive Style of Road Racing. The defensive rider is many times one who has no team to speak of and yet is able to get a few members together to "go bring back the break-aways." This rider is always wary and watching for attempted breaks, and is always near the front of the pack. He more or less tries to control the speed of the pack, keeping it from hard jamming or successful breaks. Although there are occasional riders who attempt this as a method of winning races, more often they are the team-mates of those who are away. They will slow the field slightly once their team has established a break, and go after any other group who are also trying to get away on their own.

In the event of puncture, this team member will stop with the member who has had the puncture and once the tire has been changed, the two riders will together unite to recapture the field. If you're on your own it's a real job to get back in the field. A puncture can be changed in about 30 seconds if you're fast. Figuring 30 feet a second if the group is doing about 28 m.p.h., he will be down 900 feet. . . . and that's if he can change his tire in 30 seconds! If you're a top notch competitor and you flat, you can bet your booties that someone in the group has initiated an attack to make it even harder for you to rejoin the field. Demoralizing, isn't it!

A final thought about gearing for road racing. In the group, higher gears can be used because the energy movement nullifies the large wind resistance factor (unless you're up front all the time). If you're in a small break-away unit, your gear choice will be lower than the group gearing by 3 or 4 points. When it comes to sprinting for the finish, you should know your best sprinting gear, and adapt it and yourself to any adverse conditions like a head wind or steep upgrade.

A refreshing pause—Courtesy Bill Olsen

Know your gears. Know how they're arranged on your bicycle. Know automatically how to change them without even a thought to what gear you're selecting. Know how to shift it smoothly so it doesn't get hung up, go off the chainwheel or into the spokes. If you need an excuse to save face from a poor performance, find one other than, "I had gear trouble!" That's the mark of a rank amateur, and yet I hear this over and over.

Feeding during the Race: In races over 50 miles, feeding to cyclists from trainers is permitted. Most cyclists carry some food with them as well as beverages in the water carrier. They carry easily digestible items such as bananas and oranges, as well as the popular food energy sticks.

The beverage is generally water, the reason for this is two-fold.

A. Some beverages are not always thirst quenchers.

B. If you're hot and want to cool off, it's not pleasant to pour orange juice over your head.

The feeding station itself is a specified area of about a half mile, somewhere past the 50 mile mark. Nobody should wait 50 miles to eat! A hearty breakfast about an hour before the race departure and then two snacks should carry the rider up to the 50 mile mark. (Don't let the "machine" run out of "gas," keep it well "fueled.")

To be "fed" requires two things. A person who

A chance to refuel—Courtesy Photoflash, Roanne, France

will feed you and an agreement on how it's to be managed.

How it's to be managed is important. If you miss your "feeder" you go hungry until the end of the race or unless a fellow competitor takes pity on you! So both you and your feeder should practice pick-ups.

1. The food to be passed on to you can be steak or chicken cut up in small pieces, broiled, of course. Even sandwiches of roast beef can be included, if packaged neatly.
2. All food is placed in a musette bag (cloth bag with fold over flap and long shoulder strap).
3. Feeder stands in an area free from other feeders, separated by at least 20 feet from other feeders. He should wear a particular bright shirt or outfit that is easily recognized by the rider he is feeding.
4. When the rider approaches, he will still be moving at about 20 m.p.h. The feeder can either:
   A. run along side the rider and hand the bag to the rider.
   B. hold the loop of the shoulder strap wide open so the rider can loop his arm right through and automatically swing the bag up on the shoulder.

Of the two, I prefer B. Practice both.

Drugs: Sooner or later you'll be hearing about the top notch Europeans "taking stimulants." Most of it is exaggeration, but there is some in both the amateur and professional circuits.

World Championship, Olympic and Pan American contestants must take a urine or saliva test immediately at the finish of an event. That cuts out alot.

We know that some drugs are stimulating and on a one try basis probably wouldn't do any harm.

However, there's a few things to think about:

A. They are *forbidden*. If you're caught, it's the end to a racing career.

B. Unless you've experimented with them, you won't know what they will do to your pattern of racing. If your timing is all off, whatever advantage they might have given you is lost.

C. On a steady basis, drugs can be addictive.

D. Drugs create the impression of unlimited physical resources. The straining athlete can do unbelievable harm to himself physically in this state. . . . even to the point of death.

In today's drug-oriented society, we don't need it in sports.

Area Racing: A listing of all competitive events for your area can be obtained from your State Representative. He can also inform you about the velodromes and their locations. You might be willing to drive the 250 to 300 miles to reach them.

Record Attempts: One of the best means of obtaining publicity is through record attempts. A listing of the records currently held is as follows:

Amateur Bicycle League of America Inc.

CHESTER NELSEN SR., *Records Chairman*
OFFICIAL COMPETITION RECORDS

OUTDOOR BANKED TRACK—UNPACED MILES vs. TIME
By Ronald Skarin, Van Nuys, Calif., Oct. 21, 1970

MILES	TIME	MILES	TIME
1	2 Min. 13.6 Sec.	7	15 Min. 39.7 Sec.
2	4 Min. 27.9 Sec.	8	17 Min. 58.8 Sec.
3	6 Min. 42.1 Sec.	9	20 Min. 11.1 Sec.
4	8 Min. 55.5 Sec.	10	22 Min. 21.4 Sec.
5	11 Min. 10.5 Sec.	11	24 Min. 43.6 Sec.
6	13 Min. 24.3 Sec.	12	27 Min. 01.0 Sec.

By Wes Chowen, Encino, Calif., July 6, 1967

MILES	TIME
13	29 Min. 27.4 Sec.
14	31 Min. 43.2 Sec.
15	38 Min. 59.2 Sec.
20	45 Min. 22.1 Sec.
25	56 Min. 48.3 Sec.
30	1 Hr. 8 Min. 24.2 Sec.

OUTDOOR BANKED TRACK—DISTANCE AGAINST TIME

MILES		TIME	NAME AND PLACE	DATE
25 M	3975 Ft.	1 Hr.	Bob Best—San Francisco, Calif.	June 12, 1960
47 M	5262 Ft.	2 Hr.	Bob Tetzlaff—Brown Deer, Wis.	Oct. 4, 1960
64 M	5245 Ft.	3 Hr.	Paul Washak—Brown Deer, Wis.	Aug. 15, 1960
84 M	2780 Ft.	4 Hr.	Paul Washak—Brown Deer, Wis.	Aug. 15, 1960
103 M	4250 Ft.	5 Hr.	Paul Washak—Brown Deer, Wis.	Aug. 15, 1960
122 M	5037 Ft.	6 Hr.	Paul Washak—Brown Deer, Wis.	Aug. 15, 1960
141 M	3409 Ft.	7 Hr.	Paul Washak—Brown Deer, Wis.	Aug. 15, 1960
159 M	3820 Ft.	8 Hr.	Paul Washak—Brown Deer, Wis.	Aug. 15, 1960
178 M	682 Ft.	9 Hr.	Paul Washak—Brown Deer, Wis.	Aug. 15, 1960
195 M	717 Ft.	10 Hr.	Paul Washak—Brown Deer, Wis.	Aug. 15, 1960
212 M	717 Ft.	11 Hr.	Paul Washak—Brown Deer, Wis.	Aug. 15, 1960
230 M	3645 Ft.	12 Hr.	Paul Washak—Brown Deer, Wis.	Aug. 15, 1960

OUTDOOR BANKED TRACK—UNPACED COMPETITION
1000 Meters 1 min. 9.7 secs.   Jackie Simes-Northbrook, Ill. July 6, 1967
*1000 Meters 1 min. 5.67 secs. Olympic Games Mexico City 1968
4000 Meters 5 min. 5.4 secs.   John Vandevelde   July 2, 1970
                                Glen Ellen, Ill.
*4000 Meters 4 min. 55.4 secs. Olympic Games Mexico City 1968
24 miles, 1962 Feet—1 Hour Steve Pfeiffer-Chicago, Ill. Sept. 3, 1959

OUTDOOR BANKED TRACK—SCRATCH COMPETITION

MILES	TIME	NAME AND PLACE	DATE
* ½	59.9 secs.	Peter Senia, Jr., Northbrook, Ill.	Aug. 21, 1966
* 2	4 mins. 42.6 secs.	Chris Rose—Northbrook, Ill.	Aug. 21, 1966
10	21 mins. 29 secs.	William Kind—Encino, Calif.	Aug. 1965

MILES	TIME		
¼	29.4 Sec.	B. W. King-Atlantic City, N.J.	Sept. 16, 1922
½	38.6 Sec.	Charles Winters-Chicago, Ill.	Sept. 8, 1923
⅔			
1	2 Min. 02 Sec.	Henry Surman	Aug. 8, 1908
1	2 Min. 02 Sec.	R. L. Guthridge-Westfield, N.J.	Aug. 8, 1908
1	2 Min. 02 Sec.	S. C. Haberle	Aug. 8, 1908
2	4 Min. 43.2 Sec.	Robert Parson-Milwaukee, Wis.	Aug. 26, 1961
3	7 Min. 18.2 Sec.	Don Sheldon-Columbus, Ohio	Aug. 18, 1946
5	11 Min. 38 Sec.	Vaughn Angell-Columbus, Ohio	Aug. 5, 1951
15	34 Min. 14.6 Sec.	Francois Mertens-Washington, D.C.	Aug. 7, 1955

20	45 Min. 22 Sec.	A. E. Wahl-Buffalo, N.Y.	July 4, 1921
25	1 Hr.02 Min. 01.4 Sec.	Rupert Waltl-Belleville, N.J.	May 8, 1955
30	1 Hr.10 Min. 48 Sec.	Francois Mertens-Washington, D.C. Aug. 7, 1935
50	1 Hr.56 Min. 10.7 Sec.	Jack Simes-Somerville, N.J.	May 30, 1967
75	3 Hr.15Min. 58 Sec.	Eddie Doerr, St. Louis, Mo.	April 23, 1972
100	4 Hr.23 Min. 45 Sec.	Donald Nelsen-St. Louis, Mo.	July 25, 1965
125	5 Hr.41 Min. 30 Sec.	Bernard Dodd-Lake Merced, Calif. Aug. 19, 1956
100km		Arnold Uhrlass-Flemington, N.J.
	2 Hr.40 Min. 11 Sec.		July 4, 1963
240.8	12 Hrs.	Ted Ernst-Pittsburgh, Pa.	Oct. 4, 1953

ROAD COMPETITION—4 MAN TEAM UNPACED
100km 2 Hr.24 Min. 00.97 Sec.   Wes Chowen, Bob Freund,
                                Michael Hiltner, Bob Tetzlaff Rome, Italy
                                —Olympics 1960

OUTDOOR BANKED TRACK—PURSUIT COMPETITION
4,000 Meters—4 Man Team, Skip Cutting, Steve Maaranen, John Van
             De Velde, Wayne Le Bombard
             4 min. 39.3 secs., Encino, Calif.   Aug. 1968
*4,000 Meters—4 Man Team, Dave Chauner, Harry Cutting, Steve
             Maaranen, John Van De Velde
             4 min. 32.87 secs. Olympic Games
             Mexico City 1968
4,000 Meters—2 Man Team, Hans Wolf, Arnold Uhrlass
             5 mins. 10.1 secs., Kissena Park,
             Flushing, N.Y.C. Sept. 1964

OUTDOOR BANKED TRACK—MATCH RACE COMPETITION
Last 200 Meters 11.4 seconds Jackie Simes, Copenhagen   June 5, 1962

OUTDOOR BANKED TRACK--UNPACED MILES vs. TIME—WOMEN
By—Audry McElmury, Encino, Calif.   July 12, 1969

MILES	TIME	MILES	TIME
2	4.52.1	11	26.31.6
3	7.16.3	12	28.58.4
4	9.40.9	13	31.23.5
5	12.05.3	14	33.50.2
6	14.29.5	15	36.17
7	16.54.7	16	48.39.7
8	19.16.5	25	60.28.4
9	21.42.5	Distance for one hour	
10	24.07.2	was 24 miles 4098 feet 9 inches	

OUTDOOR BANKED TRACK—WOMEN'S RECORDS
200 Meters Flying Start 13.3 secs. Edith Johnson, Northbrook, Ill.
                                                      Aug. 1965
½ Mile 1 min. 3.5 secs. Edith Johnson, Brown Deer, Wis. Aug. 26, 1961
1 Mile 2 min. 20.9 secs. Nancy Burghart, St. Louis, Mo. Aug. 26, 1962
2 Mile 5 min. 6 secs. Elizabeth Burghart, St. Louis, Mo. Aug. 26, 1962
3,000 Meters 4 min. 08.2 secs. Audrey McElmury, Encino, Calif.
                                                      July 7, 1968

* ASTERISK—HIGH ALTITUDE RECORD, NOT OFFICIAL

ROAD COMPETITION—HANDICAP

MILES   TIME
3   7 Min. 21 Sec. Jerome Steinert-Rye Beach N.Y.
                                 Sept. 12, 1909
5   12 Min. 28.4 Sec. J. B. Hawkins-Valley Stream, N.Y.
                                 Nov. 8, 1908
10   23 Min. 08 Sec. Tom Bello-Floral Park, N.Y. Sept. 12, 1909
13   30 Min. 56.6 Sec. Eugene Aickelin-Bronx, N.Y. May 20, 1923
15   34 Min. 52.8 Sec. Eugene Aickelin-Brooklyn, N.Y.
                                 June 24, 1923
20   49 Min. 55 Sec. Glenn A. Baxter-San Bernardino, Calif.
                                 May 12, 1917
25   57 Min. 15 Sec. Bernard Dodd-Oakland, Calif. Oct. 14, 1956
50 1 Hr.58 Min. 05.6 Sec. Karl Napper-Commack, L.I., N.Y.
                                 May 7, 1961
60 2 Hr.17 Min. 38 Sec. William Yarwood-Camden to
                     Atlantic Ct.   June 10, 1923
100 4 Hr.05 Min. 44 Sec. Francois Mertens-Wesbury, N.Y.
                                 June 8, 1952

ROAD COMPETITION—UNPACED

1   2 Min. 8 Sec. Berthold Baker-Grant City, N.J.
                                 Oct. 11, 1914
10M   23 Min.02.4 Sec. Mike Neel, Oakland, Calif. Aug. 15, 1971
25   58 Min. 5 Sec. Wm. Kund-Riverside, Calif.   Mar. 1965
60 2 Hr.35 Min. 9 Sec. John Sinibaldi-Paterson, N.J. June 9, 1935
90 4 Hr.23 Min. 58 Sec. Albert Marquart-Paterson, N.J. June 9, 1929
150 8 Hr.26 Min. 27 Sec. Joseph Kopsky-Floral Park, N.Y.
                                 May 5, 1912

WOMEN'S ROAD RECORDS

25 Mile Scratch—1 Hr. 4 Mins. 44 Secs. Audrey McElmury,
            Riverside, Calif.   April 1966
12 Hours Scratch—217.4 Miles—Ruth Sibley, Pittsburgh, Pa.
                                 Oct. 14, 1953

*These records marked with asterisk placed new in 1967 Book

The Records Chairman has a standard information sheet for the items needed to make an attempt on any of these records. The President of the ABL of A will forward you his name and address.

Past National Champions:

YEAR	HELD AT	SENIOR	JUNIOR	WOMEN
1921	Washington, D.C.	Arthur Nieminsky, N.Y.	None	None
1922	Atlantic City, N.J.	Carl Hambacher, N.J.	Charles Smithson, D of C	None
1923	Chicago, Ill.	Charles Barclay, Calif.	Samuel Dowell, Ohio	None
1924	Buffalo, N.Y.	Charlie Winter, N.Y.	William Honeman, N.J.	None
1925	St. Louis, Mo.	Edward Merkner, Ill.	Walter Bresnan, N.Y.	None
1926	Philadelphia, Pa.	Edward Merkner, Ill.	Charles Atwood, D of C	None
1927	Louisville, Ky.	Jimmy Walthour, N.Y.	Ted Becker, Ill.	None
1928	Kenosha, Wisc.	R. J. Connor, D of C	Bobby Thomas, Wisc.	None
1929	Newark, N.J.	Serglo Matteini, N.Y.	Tino Reboli, N.J.	None
1930	Kenosha, Wisc.	Bobby Thomas, Wisc.	George Thomas, Wisc.	None
1935	Atlantic City, N.J.	Cecil Hursey, Ca.	David Martin, N.J.	None
1936	St. Louis, Mo.	Jackie Simes, N.J.	David Martin, N.J.	None
1937	Buffalo, N.Y.	Charles Bergna, N.J.	Furman Kugler, N.J.	Doris Kopsky, N.J.
1939	Columbus, Ohio	Martin Deras, Calif.	Frank Paul, Utah	Gladys Owen, N.Y.
1940	Detroit, Mich.	Furman Kugler, N.J.	Harry Naismyth, N.J.	Mildred Kugler, N.J.
1941	Pasadena, Calif.	Marvin Thomson, Ill.	Andres Bernardsky, Calif.	Jean Michels, Ill.
1945	Chicago, Ill.	Ted Smith, N.Y.	Spencer Busch, N.Y.	Mildred Dietz, Mo.
1946	Columbus, Ohio	Don Hester, Calif.	Don Sheldon, N.J.	Mildred Dietz, Mo.
1947	Philadelphia, Pa.	Ted Smith, N.Y.	Joe Cirone, Calif.	Doris Travani, Mich.
1948	Kenosha, Wisc.	Ted Smith, N.Y.	Donald Clausen, Wisc.	Doris Travani, Mich.
1949	San Diego, Calif.	James Lauf, Md.	Donald Clausen, Wisc.	Doris Travani, Mich.
1950	New Brunswick, N.J.	Robert Pfarr, Wisc.	Harry Backer, Calif.	Doris Travani, Mich.
1951	Columbus, Ohio	Gus Gatto, Calif.	Vaughn Angell, Utah	Anna Piplak, Ill.
1952	New Brunswick, N.J.	Steven Hromjak, Ohio	John Chiselko, N.J.	Jeanne Robinson, Mich.
1953	St. Louis, Mo.	Ronnie Rhoads, Calif.	Jack Hartman, Calif.	Nancy Neiman, Mich.
1954	Minneapolis, Minn.	Jack Disney, Calif.	Robert Zumwalt, Jr.	Nancy Neiman, Mich.
1955	New York, N.Y.	Jack Disney, Calif.	Pat DeCollibus, N.Y.	Jeanne Robinson, Mich.
1956	Orlando, Fla.	Jack Disney, Calif.	Dave Staub, Calif.	Nancy Neiman, Mich.
1957	Kenosha, Wisc.	Jack Disney, Calif.	Perry Metzler, Calif.	Nancy Neiman, Mich.
1958	Newark, N.J.	Jack Disney, Calif.	James Donovan, N.Y.	Maxine Conover, Wash.
1959	Kenosha, Wisc.	James Rossi, Ill.	Jackie Simes 3rd, N.J.	Joanne Speckin, Mich.
1960	Milwaukee, Wisc.	James Rossi, Ill.	Bobbie Fenn, N.Y.	Edith A. Johnson, N.Y.
1961	Milwaukee, Wisc.	James Rossi, Ill.	Alan Grieco, N.J.	Edith A. Johnson, N.Y.
1962	St. Louis, Mo.	James Rossi, Ill.	Alan Grieco, N.J.	Nancy Burghart, N.Y.
1963	Chicago, Ill.	James Rossi, Ill.	Jose Nin, N.Y.	Edith Johnson, N.Y.
1964	New York, N.Y.	Jackie Simes, N.J.	Tom McMillan, Calif.	Nancy Burghart, N.Y.
1965	Encino, Calif.	Jack Simes, N.J. Sprint Harry Cutting, Calif. Pursuit William Kund, Calif. 10 Mile Michael Hiltner, Calif. Road	Peter Senia, N.Y.	Nancy Burghart, N.Y.
1966	Clarksville, Mo.	Don Nelson, Mo. 100 Kilometer		
1966	Northbrook, Ill.	Jack Disney, Calif. Sprint Dave Brink, Calif. Pursuit Jim Rossi, Ill. 10 Mile Robert Tetzlaff, Calif. Road	Dave Johnson, Wisc.	Edith Johnson, Sprint Audrey Mc Elmury, Pursuit Audrey Mc Elmury, Road
1967	Portland, Oregon	Jack Simes, N.J. Sprint Dave Brink, No. Calif. Pursuit Steven Maaranen, Ore. 10 Mile Bob Parsons, No. Calif. Road	Peter Senia, Jr., N.Y. Track Jim Van Boven, Road Belmont, Calif.	Nancy Burghart, N.Y. Sprint Nancy Burghart, N.Y. Pursuit Nancy Burghart, N.Y. Road
1968	Encino, Calif.	Jack Disney, Calif. Sprint Dave Brink, Calif. Pursuit Steve Maaranen, Ore. 10 Mile John Howard, Missouri, Road	Gary Campbell, Calif. Track Tracy Wakefield, Calif. Road	Nancy Burghart, N.Y. Sprint Nancy Burghart, N.Y. Pursuit Nancy Burghart, N.Y. Road
1969	Detroit, Mich.	Tim Mountford, Calif. Sprint John Vande Velde, Ill. Pursuit Jack Simes, U.S. Army, 10 Mile Alan De Fever, Calif. Road	Gary Campbell, Calif. Sprint Don Westell, N.Y. Road	Audrey Mc Elmury, Calif. Track and Road Top Point Score
1970	New York, N.Y.	Harry Cutting, Calif. Sprint John Vande Velde, Ill. Pursuit Bob Phillips, Maryland, 10 Mile Mike Carnahan, N.Y.	Jesus Portalatin, N.Y. Sprint Henry Whitney, Virginia Road	Audrey Mc Elmury, Calif. Pursuit Jeanne Kloska, N.Y. Sprint Audrey Mc Elmury, Calif. Road
1971	Portland, Oregon	Gary Campbell, Calif. Sprint Mike Neel, Calif. Pursuit Hans Neurenberg, Wisc. 10 Mile Tim Zasadny, Ill. 1000 Meter Steve Dayton, Ind. Road	Ralph Therrio, Calif. Track Ralph Therrio, Calif. Road	Sheila Young, Sprint Kathy Eckroth, Pursuit Mary Jane Reoch, Road
1972	Kenosha-Milwaukee, Wisc.	Gary Campbell, Calif. Sprint John Vande Velde, Ill. Pursuit Bob Phillips, Md. 10 Mile Steve Woznick, Fla. 1000 Meter John Howard, Mo. Road Andre Berclaz, N.Y. Veteran-Road	Nelson Saldana, N.Y. Track Ted Waterbury, Ohio, Road	Sue Novara, Mich. Sprint Clara Teyssier, Calif. Pursuit Debbie Bradley, Iowa, Road

Car Top Carriers: Sooner or later the touring or racing athlete will need a car top carrier. The three that I am familiar with are most adequate. Two can be obtained from the CYCLO-PEDIA COMPANY.

1. Bumper mount bike carrier. Under $15.00
2. Twin Bike Carrier. Under $30.00

Twin Bike Carrier

One of the most popular models is a do-it-yourself multi-bike carrier for clubs who have 3 or 4 riders travelling to races. The plans for this model can be obtained from "Chick" Mead, Marion, Massachusetts, a very dedicated bicycle dealer who really digs touring.

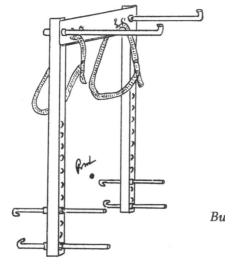

Bumper Mount Bicycle Carrier

Chick Meade's Popular Do-it-yourself bicycle carrier

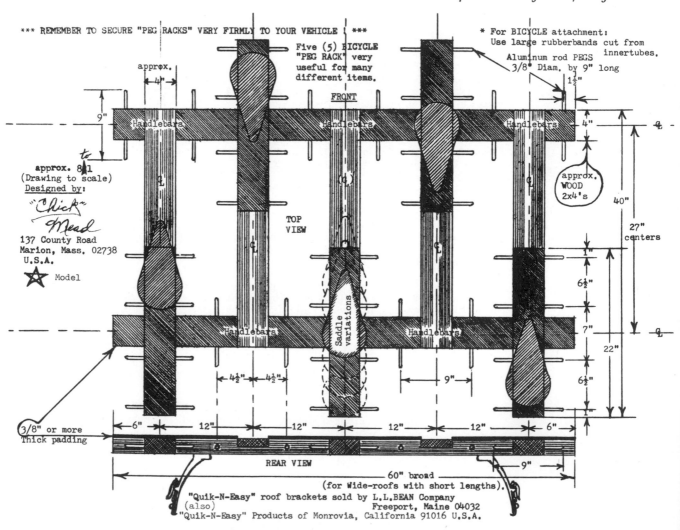

*** REMEMBER TO SECURE "PEG RACKS" VERY FIRMLY TO YOUR VEHICLE ! ***

Five (5) BICYCLE "PEG RACK" very useful for many different items.

FRONT

* For BICYCLE attachment:
Use large rubberbands cut from innertubes.
Aluminum rod PEGS 3/8" Diam. by 9" long

approx. 4"

9"

Handlebars.   Handlebars.   Handlebars.   4"

approx. 8:1 (Drawing to scale)
Designed by:

"Chick"
Mead
137 County Road
Marion, Mass. 02738
U.S.A.

★ Model

TOP VIEW

approx. WOOD 2x4's

40"

27" centers

1"

6½"

Saddle variations

Handlebars   Handlebars   7"

22"

4½" 4½"   9"   6½"

1"

3/8" or more Thick padding

6"   12"   12"   12"   12"   6"

REAR VIEW

9"

60" broad
(for Wide-roofs with short lengths).

"Quik-N-Easy" roof brackets sold by L.L.BEAN Company
(also)   Freeport, Maine 04032
"Quik-N-Easy" Products of Monrovia, California 91016 U.S.A.

GEAR RATIOS

SPROCKET	13		14		15		16		17		18		19		20		21		22	
WHEEL DIA. CHAINWHEEL	26"	27"	26"	27"	26"	27"	26"	27"	26"	27"	26"	27"	26"	27"	26"	27"	26"	27"	26"	27"
30	60	62.3	55.7	57.8	52	54	48.7	50.6	45.8	47.6	43.3	45	41	42.6	39	40.5	37.1	38.6	35.4	36.8
31	62	64.2	57.6	59.7	53.7	55.8	50.4	52.3	47.4	49.2	44.8	46.5	42.4	44	40.3	41.8	38.4	39.8	36.6	38
32	64	66.4	59.5	61.7	55.6	57.6	52	54	49	50.8	46.2	48	43.8	45.5	41.6	43.2	39.7	41.1	37.9	41.1
33	66	68.5	61.3	63.6	57.2	59.4	53.6	55.6	50.5	52.4	47.7	49.5	45.2	46.8	42.9	44.5	40.9	42.4	39	40.5
34	68	70.6	63.1	65.5	59	61.1	55.2	57.2	52	54	49.2	51	46.5	48.2	44.2	45.9	42	43.7	40.2	41.6
35	70	71.9	65	67.5	60.7	63	56.9	59	53.5	55.5	50.6	52.5	47.9	49.2	45.5	47.2	43.3	45	41.4	42.9
36	72	74.7	66.8	69.5	62.4	64.8	58.5	60.9	55	57.2	52	54	49.2	51.1	46.7	48.7	44.5	46.4	42.5	44.2
37	74	76.9	68.7	71.3	64.1	66.6	60.1	62.4	56.6	58.7	53.4	55.5	50.6	52.5	48.1	50	45.8	47.5	43.7	45.8
38	76	78.9	70	73.3	65.9	68.4	61.8	64.1	58.1	60.3	54.9	57	52	54	49.4	51.3	47.1	48.9	44.9	46.6
39	78	81	72.4	75.2	67.6	70.2	63.4	65.8	59.6	61.9	56.3	58.5	53.4	55.4	50.7	52.6	48.3	50.1	46.1	47.9
40	80	83.1	74.3	77.1	69.3	72	65	67.5	61.2	63.5	57.8	60	54.7	56.8	52	54	49.5	51.4	47.3	49.1
41	82	85.1	76.1	79	71.1	73.8	66.6	69.1	62.7	65.1	59.2	61.5	56.1	58.2	53.3	55.3	50.8	52.7	48.5	50.3
42	84	87.2	78	81	72.8	75.6	68.3	70.9	64.2	66.7	60.6	63	57.5	59.7	54.6	56.7	52	54	49.6	51.5
43	86	89.3	79.9	82.9	74.5	77.4	69.9	72.5	65.8	68.2	62.1	64.4	58.8	61.1	55.9	58.1	53.2	55.2	50.8	52.8
44	88	91.4	81.7	84.9	76.3	79.2	71.5	74.3	67.3	69.9	63.6	66	60.2	62.5	57.2	59.4	54.5	56.6	52	54
45	90	93.4	83.5	86.7	78	80.9	73.1	76	68.8	71.5	65	67.5	61.7	64	58.5	60.8	55.8	57.9	53.1	55.2
46	92	95.5	85.4	88.7	79.7	82.8	74.6	77.6	70.4	73.1	66.4	69	62.9	65.4	59.8	62.1	57	59.1	54.4	56.5
47	94	97.6	87.3	90.6	81.5	84.6	76.4	79.3	71.9	74.6	67.9	70.5	64.3	66.8	61.1	63.5	58.2	60.4	55.5	57.6
48	96	99.7	89.1	92.6	83.2	86.4	78	81	73.4	76.2	69.3	72	65.7	68.2	62.4	64.8	59.4	61.7	56.7	58.9
49	98	101.8	91	94.5	84.9	88.2	79.6	82.7	74.9	77.8	70.7	73.5	67	69.6	63.7	66.2	60.6	63	57.9	60.1
50	100	103.9	92.9	96.4	86.7	90	81.3	84.4	76.5	79.4	72.2	75	68.4	71.1	65	67.5	61.9	64.3	59.1	61.4
51	102	105.3	94.1	98.4	88.6	91.8	82.1	86.1	78	81	73.1	76.5	69.1	72.5	66.6	68.8	63.3	65.6	60.6	62.6
52	104	108	96.6	100.3	90.1	93.6	84.5	87.8	79.5	82.6	75.1	78	71.2	73.9	67.6	70.2	64.4	66.9	61.5	63.8
53	106	110	98.4	102.2	91.8	95.4	86.1	89.4	81	84.1	76.5	79.5	72.5	75.3	68.9	71.5	65.6	68.1	62.6	65
54	108	112.1	100.3	104.1	93.6	97.2	87.7	91.1	82.5	85.7	78	81	73.9	76.7	70.2	72.9	66.8	69.4	63.8	66.2
55	110	114.2	102.1	106	95.3	99	89.3	92.8	84.1	87.3	79.4	82.5	75.2	78.1	71.5	74.5	68	70.7	65	67.5
56	112	116.3	104	108	97	100.8	91	94.5	85.6	88.9	80.8	84	76.6	79.5	72.8	75.6	69.3	72	66.1	68.7

SPROCKET	23		24		25		26		27		28		29		30		31	
	26"	27"	26"	27"	26"	27"	26"	27"	26"	27"	26"	27"	26"	27"	26"	27"	26"	27"
30	33.9	35.2	32.5	33.7	31.2	32.4	30	31.1	28.9	30	27.8	28.9	26.9	27.9	26	27	25.2	26.1
31	35	36.4	33.6	34.8	32.2	33.4	31	32.1	29.9	31	28.8	29.8	27.8	28.8	26.9	27.9	26	27
32	36.2	37.5	34.7	36	33.4	34.6	32	33.2	30.8	32	29.7	30.8	28.7	29.7	27.7	28.8	26.8	27.9
33	37.3	38.7	35.8	37.1	34.3	35.6	33	34.2	31.8	33	30.6	31.8	29.6	30.7	28.6	29.7	27.7	28.7
34	38.4	39.9	36.8	38.2	35.4	36.7	34	35.3	32.7	34	31.6	32.7	30.5	31.6	29.5	30.6	28.5	29.6
35	39.6	41	37.8	39.3	36.4	37.8	35	36.3	33.7	35	32.5	33.7	31.4	32.5	30	31.5	29.4	30.5
36	40.6	42.2	39	40.5	37.4	38.8	36	37.3	34.7	36	33.4	34.7	32.3	33.5	31.2	32.4	30.2	31.4
37	41.8	43.4	40.1	41.6	38.5	40	37	38.4	35.6	37	34.4	35.6	33.2	34.4	32.1	33.3	31	32.2
38	43	44.6	41.2	42.7	39.5	41	38	39.4	36.6	38	35.3	36.6	34.1	35.3	32.9	34.2	31.9	33.1
39	44.1	45.8	42.2	43.9	40.6	42.1	39	40.5	37.6	39	36.2	37.6	35	36.3	33.8	35.1	32.7	34
40	45.2	47	43.3	45	41.6	43.2	40	41.5	38.5	40	37.1	38.6	35.9	37.2	34.7	36	33.5	34.8
41	46.3	48.1	44.4	46.1	42.6	44.2	41	42.4	39.5	41	38	39.5	36.8	38.1	35.5	36.9	34.4	35.7
42	47.5	49.3	45.5	47.2	43.7	45.3	42	43.6	40.4	42	39	40.5	37.7	39.1	36.4	37.8	35.2	36.6
43	48.6	50.4	46.6	48.3	44.7	46.4	43	44.6	41.4	43	39.9	41.4	38.6	40	37.3	38.7	36.1	37.5
44	49.8	51.6	47.7	49.5	45.8	47.5	44	45.7	42.4	44	40.9	42.4	39.4	40.9	38.1	39.6	36.9	38.4
45	50.8	52.8	48.6	50.7	46.9	48.6	45	46.7	43.3	45	41.8	43.4	40.3	41.8	39	40.5	37.7	39.2
46	52	54	49.9	51.8	47.8	49.7	46	47.8	44.3	46	42.7	44.4	41.2	42.8	39.9	41.4	38.6	40.1
47	53.1	55.2	50.9	52.9	48.9	50.8	47	48.8	45.3	47	43.6	45.3	42.1	43.4	40.7	42.3	39.4	40.9
48	54.3	56.3	52	54	49.9	51.8	48	49.9	46.2	48	44.6	46.5	43	44.6	41.6	43.2	40.3	41.8
49	55.4	57.5	53.1	55.1	51	52.9	49	50.9	47.2	49	45.5	47.2	44	45.6	42.5	44.1	41.1	42.7
50	56.5	58.7	54.2	56.3	52	54	50	51.9	48.5	50	46.4	48.2	44.8	46.5	43.3	45	41.9	43.6
51	57.7	59.9	55.3	57.4	53	55.1	51	53	49.1	51	47.4	49.2	45.7	47.4	44.2	45.9	42.5	44.4
52	58.8	61	56.3	58.5	54.1	56.2	52	54	50	52	48.3	50.1	46.6	48.4	45	46.8	43.6	45.3
53	59.9	62.2	57.4	59.6	55.1	57.2	53	55	51	53	49.2	51.1	47.5	49.3	45.9	47.7	44.5	46.2
54	61	63.3	58.5	60.7	56.1	58.3	54	56	52	54	50.1	52	48.4	50.2	46.8	48.6	45.3	47
55	62.1	64.5	59.5	61.8	57.2	59.4	55	57.1	53	55	51	53	49.3	51.2	47.7	49.5	46.1	47.9
56	63.3	65.7	60.6	63	58.2	60.4	56	58.1	53.9	56	52	54	50.2	52.1	48.5	50.4	47	48.8

* TO COMPUTE RATIOS NOT GIVEN ON THIS CHART, TAKE THE DIAMETER OF THE REAR WHEEL IN INCHES, MULTIPLY BY THE NUMBER OF TEETH IN THE FRONT CHAINWHEEL, AND DIVIDE BY THE NUMBER OF TEETH ON THE REAR SPROCKET.

* WHEN SELECTING RATIOS FOR YOUR CYCLE, MAKE CERTAIN THAT THE DERAILLEUR MECHANISM HAS THE CAPACITY TO WORK WITH THE RATIOS SELECTED.

Gear Ratio Listing—Courtesy Gene Portuesi's CycloPedia

GEAR RATIO	REVOLUTIONS PER MINUTE OF THE CRANK ARM										
	60	75	80	90	100	120	130	140	150	160	
30	5.37	6.7	7.5	8.05	8.95	10.7	11.6	12.5	13.4	14.3	MPH
32	5.71	7.5	7.65	8.6	9.55	11.45	12.04	13.35	14.3	15.25	MPH
34	6.0	7.65	8.15	9.1	10.15	12.15	13.2	14.2	15.25	16.2	MPH
36	6.4	8.0	8.5	9.65	10.75	12.53	13.95	15.0	16.1	17.2	MPH
38	6.8	8.5	9.06	10.2	11.4	13.6	14.7	15.85	17.0	18.2	MPH
40	7.15	8.95	9.55	10.7	11.95	14.3	15.5	16.7	17.8	19.1	MPH
42	7.50	9.40	10.0	11.25	12.55	15.0	16.30	17.5	18.7	20.1	MPH
44	7.85	9.85	10.5	11.8	13.15	15.7	17.0	18.3	19.6	21.0	MPH
46	8.21	10.3	11.0	12.32	13.72	16.4	17.8	19.2	20.5	22.0	MPH
48	8.51	10.72	11.45	12.88	14.32	17.15	18.6	20.0	21.40	22.9	MPH
50	8.94	11.2	11.9	13.4	14.9	17.9	19.4	20.8	22.3	23.85	MPH
52	9.3	11.68	12.4	13.95	15.5	18.5	20.2	21.65	23.2	24.9	MPH
54	9.65	12.1	12.9	14.5	16.2	19.3	20.9	22.5	24.1	25.9	MPH
56	10.0	12.5	13.4	15.0	16.7	20.0	21.7	23.4	25.0	26.75	MPH
58	10.36	12.95	13.82	15.55	17.3	20.7	22.5	24.2	25.9	27.6	MPH
60	10.75	13.4	14.3	16.1	17.9	21.4	23.25	25.0	26.8	28.7	MPH
62	11.1	13.85	14.8	16.6	18.5	22.2	24.0	25.85	27.7	29.6	MPH
64	11.43	14.3	15.3	17.2	19.1	22.9	24.8	26.7	28.6	30.5	MPH
66	11.8	14.64	15.65	17.7	19.7	23.6	25.6	27.5	29.6	31.5	MPH
68	12.12	15.2	16.3	18.2	20.3	24.3	26.4	28.4	30.5	32.45	MPH
70	12.51	15.65	16.7	18.75	21.0	25.0	27.1	29.2	31.3	33.4	MPH
72	12.87	16.1	17.2	19.3	21.5	25.7	27.9	30.0	32.2	34.4	MPH
74	13.2	16.58	17.7	19.8	22.1	26.55	28.7	30.9	33.0	35.3	MPH
76	13.6	17.0	18.1	20.4	22.7	27.2	29.4	31.7	34.0	36.3	MPH
78	13.9	17.4	18.6	20.9	23.4	27.9	30.2	32.6	34.8	37.2	MPH
80	14.3	17.9	19.1	21.45	23.9	28.6	31.0	33.3	35.8	38.2	MPH
82	14.62	18.35	19.5	22.0	24.5	29.4	31.8	34.2	36.65	39.1	MPH
84	15.0	18.8	20.0	22.6	25.1	30.0	32.6	35.0	37.6	40.0	MPH
86	15.4	19.2	20.55	23.0	25.75	30.7	33.4	35.9	38.4	41.1	MPH
88	15.7	19.7	21.0	23.6	26.3	31.5	34.15	36.8	39.3	42.0	MPH
90	16.1	20.2	21.5	24.2	27.0	32.2	34.8	37.5	40.2	43.0	MPH
92	16.44	20.6	22.0	24.65	27.45	32.8	35.6	38.3	41.3	43.9	MPH
94	16.8	21.0	22.45	25.2	28.1	33.6	36.4	39.2	42.0	44.9	MPH
96	17.15	21.5	22.95	25.75	28.7	34.3	37.2	40.0	42.8	45.8	MPH
98	17.5	21.9	23.4	26.2	29.25	35.0	38.0	40.8	43.8	46.7	MPH
100	17.9	22.4	23.9	26.8	29.95	35.75	38.8	41.7	44.8	47.8	MPH
102	18.2	22.8	24.4	27.3	30.45	36.55	39.6	42.6	45.7	48.8	MPH
104	18.6	23.25	24.85	27.9	31.0	37.25	40.4	43.4	46.7	49.6	MPH
106	18.9	23.7	25.3	28.4	31.3	37.9	41.3	44.2	47.5	50.6	MPH

CYCLO-PEDIA Cadence Chart.   Calibrated by Professor Paul R. "Pop" Kepner.

Cadence Listing—Courtesy Gene Portuesi's Cyclo-Pedia

17

Cycling While in the Military Service

Special Services is available to outstanding cyclists who are serving their country in military service during Pan American and Olympic years. To begin with:

1. Keep a record of all your past achievements. Before entering the service ask for a letter of reference from your local State Representative, Board of Director Member, Mayor, State Senator and Governor.

   a. Make at least six copies of each item.

2. Write to the President of the ABL of A for the address of the Olympic Cycling Chairman. When you receive this, send him one copy of your achievement record, and reference letters, notifying him that you are applying for a transfer to Special Services, and your Commanding Officer's name.

3. With three copies of your achievement record and reference letters, write your Commanding Officer requesting placement in special services. Send a fourth copy of this letter and one copy of the achievement record to the Adjutant General's Office.

4. If you don't receive a reply from your Commanding Officer in 3 weeks, write a follow-up letter with a copy to the Olympic Committee. It takes approximately 6 or 7 weeks to process the transfer. Remember that a well written letter many times impresses everyone and instills in those who receive it the thought that this fine young man can really bring credit to his branch of the armed services.

There are cases where very glib-tongued average cyclists have received placement and other most deserving athletes have not. Fortunately this doesn't occur too often.

After the application has been approved, the cyclist will be transferred to a base nearby one of the larger cycling centers that has been chosen to house the cycling branch of Special Services. They are usually given a vehicle for transportation and receive very special and excellent treatment allowing them to train and compete as they program. This service team will then be sent to the site of the trials and billeted within the area.

If the riders place on the actual Pan American or Olympic Team they will receive additional consideration from the services. Those who do not make the team are then returned to their regular outfits to continue their tour of duty.

Occasionally a rider might receive special consideration from his Commanding Officer and the ABL of A to compete in the annual World Championships, or other important cycling events. This is not a unified service team effort and success of this request is largely a matter of luck. If there is a great deal of military unrest throughout the world it is very doubtful if a release can be obtained.

After competing in the actual Pan American or Olympic races, these special service riders are then returned to their regular outfits to continue their tour of duty.

Any printed publicity should be clipped, photographed and sent to the Commanding Officer, with a copy to the Adjutant General and the ABL of A Olympic Committee Chairman. Make it a point to see that there *is* publicity. Wherever you're located, contact the sports editor of the local paper and tell him about your services team. They'll thank you for giving them an extra angle to work on and it impresses those who have supported you. It also paves the way toward getting extra time off to go to some local events and even training.

Epilogue

Whatever your age or temperament, the unlimited world of cycling has something for everyone. Whether it's an escape from the office, home, school or factory that has sent you cycling, the healthful aspects can be matched by the freedom it provides.

Make it a part of your daily routine, and let it bring into your life a spiritual release that can serve you forever.

Bibliography

BOOKS

Baranet, Nancy Neiman. *The Turned Down Bar*. Philadelphia: Dorrance & Company, 1964.

Encyclopedia Britannica. "Bicycle." Wm. Benton Publisher, 1967.

Meiffret, Jose. *Mes Rendez-Vous la Mort*. Paris, France: Flammarion, 1964.

Morehouse, Laurence E., and Augustus T. Miller. *The Physiology of Exercise*. St. Louis: C. V. Mosby Company, 1967.

Nolan, William F. *Barney Oldfield*. New York: G. P. Putnam's Sons, 1961.

Palmer, Arthur Judson. *Riding High*. New York: E. P. Dutton Co.

Taylor, Marshall W. "Major". *The Fastest Bicycle Rider in the World*. Worcester, Mass.: Wormley Publishing Company, 1928.

PAMPHLETS

Bike Racing on Campus. New York: Bicycle Institute of America (122 E. 42nd St., New York 17, N.Y.)

Bike Trails and Facilities. New York: Bicycle Institute of America.

Cycling Almanac, Otto Eisele's. New York: 1950 to 1953.

Cycling in the School Fitness Program. Washington, D.C.: American Association for Health, Physical Education and Recreation, 1963.

Cyclo-Pedia, Gene Portuesi's. Cadillac, Michigan: Cycle Sport Shop, 1971.

The Family Hosteling Manual. New York: American Youth Hostels, Inc.

Handbook on Bicycle Tracks and Cycle Racing. Dayton, Ohio: The Huffman Manufacturing Company, 1965.

Harper's Weekly, New York: Issues 1886 to 1897.

Smithsonian Institute, Washington, D.C.: Bulletin #204. 1955.

ARTICLES

Kepner, Paul R. "Cadence Chart." *Cyclo-Pedia*, 1971, Page 52.

Portuesi, Eugene G. "Gear Ratios." *Cyclo-Pedia*, 1971, Page 53.

White, Dr. Paul Dudley. "For Fun and Fitness, Get Back on a Bike." New York: Bicycle Institute of America.

Index